Exploring the Future

Seven Strategic Conversations that Could Transform Your Association

ALSO AVAILABLE FROM THE ASAE FOUNDATION

Exploring the Future

Seven Strategic Conversations that Could Transform Your Association

Robert Olson and Atul Dighe

asae | american society of association executives

FOUNDATION

asae | american society of association executives

Washington, DC

Information in this book is accurate as of the time of publication and consistent with standards of good practice in the general management community. As research and practice advance, however, standards may change. For this reason, it is recommended that readers evaluate the applicability of any recommendation in light of particular situations and changing standards.

American Society of Association Executives
1575 I Street, NW
Washington, DC 20005-1103
Phone: (202) 626-2723
Fax: (202) 408-9634
E-mail: books@asaenet.org

ASAE's core purpose is to advance the value of voluntary associations to society and to support the professionalism of the individuals who lead them.

Sarah C. Varner, Executive Vice President, ASAE Foundation
Michelle Mason, Vice President, ASAE Foundation Research Programs
Erica Davis, Assistant, ASAE Foundation Research Programs

Susan Robertson, Vice President, ASAE Marketing and Communications
Anna Nunan, Director of Book Publishing
Louise Quinn, Acquisitions Coordinator
Jennifer Moon, Production Manager
Anthony Conley, Operations Coordinator
Sandra R. Sabo, Editor

Cover and interior design by Design Consultants

This book is available at a special discount when ordered in bulk quantities. For information, contact the ASAE Member Service Center at (202) 371-0940.

A complete catalog of titles is available on the ASAE Web site at www.asaenet.org/bookstore

Library of Congress Cataloging-in-Publication Data

Olson, Robert L. (Robert Linus), 1942-
    Exploring the future: seven strategic conversations that could transform your association / Robert Olson and Atul Dighe.
        p. cm.
    Includes bibliographical references.
    ISBN 0-88034-198-X
        1. Nonprofit organizations—Management. 2. Nonprofit organizations—Planning.
    3. Associations, institutions, etc.—Management. 4. Associations, institutions, etc.—Planning. 5. Societies—Management. 6. Societies—Planning. 7. Twenty-first century—Forecast. I. Dighe, Atul. II. Title.

HD62.6.O47 2001
658'.048—dc21

Printed in the United States of America.

10 9 8 7 6 5 4 3 2 1

Contents

Foreword

Adapt or die.

—Charles Darwin

When Darwin wrote those words, he was referring to survival of the species, but his comment applies today to the survival of associations. If you are hoping to take your organization very far into the new millennium, you must begin now to examine every service you provide, every program you create, every member you recruit with an eye to the future. Associations that fail to anticipate trends, create new relationships, and develop flexible and insightful leadership will find themselves struggling to survive.

There is no single formula for creating this new association. The information in this book will help you begin a dialogue with boards, staff, and volunteers that will help you design a healthy, vital organization. You must also remember that this new model must not remain static once it has been created. It should evolve and change almost organically as internal and external factors affect it. There is no single solution, design, or structure for your association.

Only one thing is certain; you cannot continue to manage your association the way you always have. If you do, it will surely become extinct. Start reading this book now—with the idea that every section will provide the ideas that help you define the discussions. The sections will help you and your organization frame the questions and discover the answers that will help you adapt to our changing environment. If your organization learns how to successfully adapt, you will not only survive, you will succeed.

D. Brent Mulgrew

Executive Director, Ohio State Medical Association

2000–2001 Chair, ASAE Foundation Environmental Scan Task Force

Preface

No matter how good you get, there's always something farther out there.

—Bill Walton

For the association community, the future has never been more uncertain. Competition is growing as emerging technologies make once-exclusive advantages, such as specialized information, widely available in the marketplace. The rate of change associations must deal with is unprecedented. That is why nonprofits must be especially resourceful today. They must look critically at their current operating environments and prepare themselves for whatever the future may bring.

The ASAE Foundation is committed to helping associations prepare for the future. The Foundation has monitored trends affecting associations since 1995. In 1998, ASAE and the ASAE Foundation partnered to conduct an extensive environmental scan of the association community to help executives understand and prepare for the trends driving change. The initial scan, *Facing the Future: A Report on Major Trends and Issues Affecting Associations*, identified fourteen trends that are affecting associations. A companion piece, *Embracing the Future: An Action Guide for Association Leaders*, gives association leaders tools to facilitate strategic thinking exercises for improving their own scanning and planning activities.

Exploring the Future: Seven Strategic Conversations that Could Transform Your Association pushes out beyond the near-certainties identified in *Facing the Future* to explore seven emerging issues that could dramatically alter the future of associations. These issues are less certain than those described in the earlier publications, but could prove to have an even greater impact. Each issue is just beginning to unfold. Each is being discussed today by thought leaders inside and outside the association community. But these issues are all in their early stages, and how they will play out over the generation ahead is still to be determined. There is no cookbook recipe for dealing with them. By initiating intentional, ongoing conversations about these issues, associations can greatly increase their chances of surviving and thriving in an era of accelerating change.

Exploring the Future is a product of the Foundation's second generation of scanning activities, called the *ASAE Foundation Futures Scan*. To look further out onto the planning horizon, the Foundation formed a partnership with the Institute for Alternative Futures, Alexandria, Virginia. The scan's cornerstone was a virtual community that used Internet-based conferencing software to conduct a ten-month-long dialogue. Participants in this virtual community included more than a hundred association executives, futurists, and guest experts. Issues identified in this online discussion were evaluated and further refined in a series of focus groups with association leaders, business partners, and consultants. The issues that emerged from this process were further refined through literature reviews and interviews with outside experts.

Taken together, *Facing the Future, Embracing the Future,* and *Exploring the Future* comprise a family of publications that you can use to navigate the currents of change and to shape a better future for your association. We are excited about the possibilities, and we are pleased to make this important contribution to our field.

Thomas C. Dolan, Ph.D., FACHE, CAE
President and CEO, American College of Healthcare Executives
2000–2001 Chair, ASAE Foundation

Acknowledgments

This report is made possible through the hard work and dedication of many individuals. The American Society of Association Executives Foundation extends its appreciation to the Institute for Alternative Futures, Alexandria, Virginia, which was commissioned by the Foundation to produce this report. Thank you to education consultant Donald R. (Chip) Levy, The Rochelle Organization, Inc., Washington, D.C., for his insights and guidance.

The ASAE Foundation also thanks the members of the 2000–01 Environmental Scan Task Force for their guidance and oversight:

Michael Anderson, CAE, President/CEO, Canadian Society of Association Executives, Toronto, Ontario, Canada

Debra Bachman-Zabloudil, CHE, CAE, Director, Education and Meetings, Association Forum, Chicago, Ill.

Jeffrey Cufaude, Principal and Partner, like minded people, Indianapolis, Ind.

Mark J. Golden, CAE, Executive Director, National Court Reporters Association, Vienna, Va.

Jery Huntly, Executive Director, Vinyl Siding Institute, Washington, D.C.

Sherry Keramidas, Ph.D., CAE, Executive Director, Regulatory Affairs Professional Society, Rockville, Md.

Robin Kriegel, CAE, CEO/Executive Director, American Society for Parenteral and Enteral Nutrition, Silver Spring, Md.

D. Brent Mulgrew (Chair), Executive Director, Ohio State Medical Association, Hilliard, Ohio

Mary Riemersma, CAE, (Co-Chair), Executive Director, California Association of Marriage and Family Therapists, San Diego, Calif.

Colin Rorrie, Jr., Ph.D, CAE, Executive Director, American College of Emergency Physicians—National Office, Dallas, Texas

Frank Schuurmans, Vice President, Professional Development, Credit Union Executives Society, Madison, Wisc.

Eve Shepard, CAE, Director, Knowledge Management, American Society of Association Executives, Washington, D.C.

Barbara Sido, CAE, Managing Director, Professional Practice, American Institute of Architects, Washington, D.C.

Introduction

It is not the answers that enlightens, but the questions.
—Decouvertes

Getting good answers about your association's future requires asking the right questions. By asking the right questions, associations will be better prepared to assert their prominence in the 21st century. The ASAE Foundation's research postulates that the right questions will start conversations that are imperative for associations to thrive in future years.

The ASAE Foundation partnered with the Institute for Alternative Futures, Alexandria, Va., to conduct a multi-year exploration of issues that associations will soon confront. In 1999, the Foundation's first environmental scan produced *Facing the Future: A Report on the Major Trends and Issues Affecting Associations*, which explored current information about emerging trends that is essential for discovering new opportunities. This publication, *Exploring the Future: Seven Strategic Conversations that Could Transform Your Association*, is about the questions that evoke action.

This publication will initiate conversations at the governance and staff levels about issues that are critical to determining the success of your organization. *Exploring the Future* identifies seven issues that should be investigated so that your organization will be prepared to adapt and thrive in the coming decades.

Seven Emerging Issues

Meaning Matters. Meaning is the best way for associations to differentiate their value to members. Associations create meaning through meaningful purpose, meaningful relationships, and meaningful contributions. Amid the chaos of rapid change, meaning and purpose are the enduring qualities that attract and retain members.

Global + Local = Glocal. "Glocalization" is a term that describes how many aspects of life are becoming more global and more local at the same time. Many national-level decisions, for example, are moving upward to international organizations and devolving downward to state and local governments. Associations will find new challenges and creative roles in a glocalizing world.

Inclusivity. A rich variety of cultural backgrounds and viewpoints within associations can improve creativity, decision-making, and programming. To tap these potentials, associations will need to shift from assimilating differences to raising awareness of differences, valuing them, and making use of them.

Generational Synergy. Achieving greater synergy among generations is one of the key challenges involved in inclusivity. Each generation has contributions to make and roles it can play in its interaction with other generations. Associations that learn to foster generational synergy will gain enormous advantages.

Learning Culture. The ability to *learn* is the single most important skill individuals and organizations need to thrive amid rapid change. Associations need to focus more on learning and less on teaching. To compete effectively with other organizations and information sources, associations need to shift from providing "continuing education" to facilitating continuous learning.

Transparency. Demands for greater openness and accountability are growing rapidly, driven by the spread of democracy, economic globalization, the digital revolution, and Internet-enhanced social activism. Associations need to balance the organizational and social advantages of greater transparency with legitimate concerns about transparency's disadvantages and limits.

Living Organizations. Instead of trying to control everything in an environment of continuous change, association leaders need to view their organizations as living systems able to self-organize to adapt to change. To promote self-organization, leaders need to clarify their purpose and values, minimize bureaucracy, and understand the critical importance of knowledge sharing and trust.

These seven strategic issues emerged from a ten-month, Internet-based futures scan discussion that involved more than a hundred association executives, futurists, and guest experts. Future-related issues were discussed in virtual and face-to-face environments. The seven issues that emerged are issues that require analysis and action. The framework will prove to be a useful tool for initiating conversations and asking the right questions to provoke leaders and staff to create opportunities for your organization's future.

The Challenge of Change

In one of the first conversations in the futures scan online dialog, futurist James Dator, president of the World Futures Studies Federation, asked participants to distribute 100 percentage points among three major drivers of change that will likely transpire over the next 20 to 50 years. You might find it interesting to make your own estimates.

_____% **Continuities**
Those things that were part of the past, are important now, and will be part of the future.

_____% **Cycles**
Economic, technological, generational, or other kinds of cycles, where things that happened before will be important again.

_____% **Novelties**
Those things that are completely new, that was not part of the past and may be emerging only now, but will be increasingly important in the future.

On average, association participants who completed Dator's online questionnaire believed that more than a third of the future will be driven by novelties; some think that as much as 50 percent of the future will be novel. On average, the futurists who responded thought that nearly two-thirds of the future will be unprecedented. Dator himself voted 80 percent for novelties.

If you look at what it is you might never attain what could be.
—Source Unknown

The idea that a third or more of the future could be radically different from today just a generation from now is novel in itself. What makes people believe that such an extraordinary rate of change is plausible? The dialog suggested three main factors.

Converging Technologies. All technologies that involve information in any way are increasingly able to interact. This is the essence of the digital revolution. Information is being reduced to the same basic form in all these systems—bits that can travel from one technology to another. Because the technologies interact, progress in one stimulates developments in the others. Information technology is fomenting technical revolutions in biotechnology, materials design, manufacturing, and many other areas. The result is an unprecedented technological acceleration.

Out farther ahead, in the 20-to-50-year range, there is less certainty but more monumental possibilities for breakthroughs in areas like nanotechnology, robotics, and artificial intelligence.

A New Economy. The explosion of knowledge and technological change is creating a new economy that is much bigger than e-commerce. While some sectors lead and others lag, the character of the whole economy is changing. It is increasingly knowledge-based, global, networked, transparent, and fast. Consumption of things is giving way to experiences, atoms to bits, possessions to relationships, and physical capital to human capital. "Matter" matters less, meaning matters more; distance is vanishing; and time is collapsing. Static rules are being replaced by faster, more flexible modes of learning and coordinating. Value chains are becoming value webs, hierarchies are flattening and linking outward, and relationships are becoming central to success.

Societal Challenges. Our society faces a wide array of challenges. Some are primarily technological. For example, improvements in energy efficiency and alternative sources of energy are needed to head off global warming and support the world economy as global oil supplies decline. Other challenges, like providing affordable health care to our aging population, or fostering more equitable patterns of global development, are primarily social. Challenges of this magnitude will require significant change to occur and has the potential to be disruptive if not dealt with appropriately.

All our experience is based on the past, but all our decisions are about the future. Accelerating change is making the past experience of association executives less relevant. This forces everyone to engage in a continuous process of learning and adaptation. Rapid change is speeding up our lives and blurring the traditional boundaries between fields and organizations. As individuals continuously change roles, learn new skills, and explore expanding options of how to live and work, their very identities—their senses of bounded, stable selves—is under siege.

The Potential for "Associating" More Effectively

The single most important requirement for operating successfully in a world of accelerating change is the ability to "associate" effectively—to bring people into more open and cooperative relationships within organizations and to form new groups and subgroups, as needed, to learn, plan, and coordinate responses to emerging developments. Many things about today's associations may eventually become obsolete, but whatever changes may come, the *process of associating* will become increasingly important.

The new economy is moving in a direction that associations have pioneered. The skills of group formation and development are critical. These skills give association leaders a head start in dealing with rapid change and helping their members meet the challenges ahead. Association members can serve as an anchor for identity in the storm of change. They can help members define who they are and how they fit in.

Associating more effectively is likely to become much easier in future years. New community tools will make it easier to bring people together, overcome barriers of time and distance, and help people carry out different tasks online, from brainstorming to decision making.

Thinking Functionally About Your Emerging Future

Exploring the Future offers two frameworks for engaging in strategic conversations about how to approach the future. You are encouraged to use the provocative questions at the conclusion of each chapter to jump-start strategic conversations with your leadership and staff.

The following grid is provided to help you think through the implications at an operational level of your organization. Your staff team should review each association function and identify how your association will respond to future opportunities.

Probe each "box" with the these questions in mind:

- What are the implications of the trend on this function?
- What actions can we take now?
- What actions should occur over the next two to three years?

Each box in the grid represents a place to write your future.

Thinking Functionally About Your Association's Future

	Meaning Matters	Inclusivity	Generational Synergy	Global+Local =Glocal	Transparency	Learning Culture	Living Organizations	
Governance								
Membership Recruitment								
Member Communications								
Accounting or Finance								
Legal Compliance								
Marketing								
Business Development								
Public Relations								
Education and Training								
Conference and Meeting Planning								
Fund Development								
Policy Making								
Governmental Affairs								
Certification								
Standards								
International								
Technology								
Chapter Relations								

SCALE: ● great impact ◐ modest impact ○ minimal impact

How to Use This Report

Exploring the Future will help focus the leadership and staff of your association as they work to meet the challenges of the future and facilitate their discovery of new opportunities. The ASAE Foundation's ongoing research reaffirms that associations need to reshape themselves and ask the right questions to remain competitive and relevant to their memberships and public. For some, these conversations may be difficult to initiate. The reality is that they need to happen.

As you read this report keep in mind that it serves two purposes:

Enables boards and staff to think, act, and ask critical questions about issues likely to impact your organization. As we enter the 21st century, there are few answers and proven techniques to help associations thrive in the future. The participants in the online futures scan discussion acknowledged that they were in a rapidly changing environment, where the questions were as important as the answers. They believe that asking the right questions and challenging assumptions will identify uncharted territory and foster new opportunities.

Facilitate dialogue and action among your leadership. Facilitating strategic conversations with key stakeholders can be a powerful resource for individual insight, community development, learning, and managing change. It will allow you to develop a stronger, more sustainable sense of community through creating shared meaning around issues that really matter. Leaders that think creatively and collectively about future impacts are able to position their organizations to be nimble and avoid costly mistakes associated with reacting too slowly.

In both cases, you can use this report as a facilitation tool to ensure that everyone starts the discussions with a shared understanding of the seven strategic conversations. Associations need to invest the time to explore the potential impacts on their organizations and fields. All participants will have the same information on hand and be able to use the same language to discuss the information.

The chapters are designed to help the boards and staff see the big picture that arises from the information extracted from the futures scan online discussion, focus groups, literature search, and other research methodologies. They also contain background information on each issue. Included in each chapter are strategic thinking tools—provocative questions and recommended resources for future exploration.

> *Strategic Conversations* are discussions that inform boards, volunteers, and staff about how to incorporate new insights on key issues into the organization's culture. The creation of new knowledge around issues and future trends likely to affect the organization will emerge to foster the development of key future strategies.

Exploring the Future concludes with additional information to keep the conversation going. A bibliography and suggested reading list offer resources for learning more about the specific issues affecting associations. Included in the appendix are excerpts from the online conversations.

CHAPTER 1
Meaning Matters

Meaning is the "why" that gives significance to all the "whats" and "hows" and helps us make sense of our lives.

The future success of associations depends on a clear purpose, strong values, and engaging opportunities for people to form meaningful relationships as they work together. These enduring qualities attract and retain members. In a world where many tangible membership benefits are merely commodities, available from multiple sources, the best way an association can differentiate its value to members is on the basis of the intangible benefit of meaning.

It took fresh competition from the for-profit world to remind associations of what has always made them special: They are organizations of people pursuing a meaningful common self-interest. That self-interest might be establishing a career for the young person or new business owner. At another stage of life it might be making business connections and gaining access to technical resources. It might become making a significant contribution to society because members want to "give back" some of what they have received.

Creating Meaning

Associations embody this human desire to affiliate and work together to create meaning. A large part of personal identity and mental and emotional well-being comes from having meaningful tasks to fulfill. Associations provide a social context in which people find others who share a common purpose and work together on meaningful tasks, creating relationships in which they are valued and respected. Intangible? Yes. Important? Unquestionably.

IMPLICATIONS FOR ASSOCIATIONS	ACTION STEPS
• People create meaning together by forming meaningful relationships to pursue meaningful purposes. • Associations have a "larger purpose" that serves society. • Meaningful contributions arise from an association's purpose. • Shared experiences, storytelling, and emotional experiences nurture meaningful relationships.	• Clarify, update, and elevate your sense of purpose, engaging people at the level of their highest aspirations. • Provide opportunities to contribute to a larger purpose for society. • Invest in strategies to accelerate the development of meaningful relationships. • Become intentional about creating shared experiences, telling stories, and evoking emotions.

Meaning and purpose can live only in the hearts and minds of members, not in the articles of incorporation or bylaws or a vision statement on a piece of paper. In times of rapid change, purposes can become obsolete or less relevant. As associations reach a mature stage of their life cycle, it is easy to fall into decline. Passions of a previous generation may fade. Industries and fields change. New understandings and priorities emerge.

As a result, you have to actively renew and create meaning. You build meaning out of the experience and traditions of your organization's past, your own understanding of the conditions and needs of the present, your beliefs, the values for which you are willing to sacrifice something, and your aspirations for the kind of future you desire for your children and the generations ahead. The ingredients are all there. Each association simply must put them together into its own unique and unifying pattern.

A strong sense of meaning is an essential reference point in making the many difficult decisions ahead. These decisions will transform not only associations but also the society in which they operate.

Meaning is like love, truth, or freedom. It's easy to get agreement that it matters, is interesting to discuss, and impossible to do anything about it unless it is grounded in tangible ways. For associations, meaning comes through purpose, relationships, stories, and contributions.

Meaning is the soul of the organization, made visible through vision, stories, connections. Meaning is developed through authentic dialogue about what's important to us. To make room for this dialogue, we have to clear away the underbrush of administrative "stuff" that boards frequently spend their time on, and engage them at a deeper, more profound level.

— **Janet G. McCallen, CAE**
Executive Director, Financial Planning Association

Meaningful Purpose

Purpose defines what your members wish to achieve by coming together. The clearer and more elevated its purpose, the more meaningful your association will be for its members and staff. Thinking about the challenges and opportunities of the future can help renew meaning and purpose in your association today.

To renew your association's sense of purpose, hold in-depth discussions on the four fundamental questions that follow.

1. *What do our current members believe the association's purpose(s) is?* Every association derives some of its sense of purpose from the primary self-interests of its members. Small business owners

may be passionate about promoting the entrepreneurial spirit or the preservation of family businesses. Members of trade associations may be primarily concerned with what they produce and having "money in our pockets." Professionals may seem to care most about regulations or reimbursement, but ask them why they chose their career and an original purpose resurfaces. In a world where stress pushes pleasure to the side, hobbyists may have the simple purpose of enjoying life.

2. *What is the association's "larger purpose"—the contributions it makes to society through its major activities?* The clearer and more elevated the larger purpose, the more meaningful your association will be for its members and staff.

In clarifying and formulating your larger purpose, reach for the most unifying theme that will bridge generations and interests. An overarching purpose avoids watering down meaning to its lowest common denominator or fracturing it into different meanings for different members. Search for an elevated aspiration that all members can identify with, regardless of where they are in their careers or their relationship with the association.

We…have to think through how to balance two apparently contradictory requirements. Organizations must competently perform the one social function for which they exist—the school to teach, the hospital to cure the sick, and the business to produce goods, services, or the capital to provide for the risks of the future…But there is also society's need for these organizations to take social responsibility—to work on the problems and challenges of the community. Together these organizations are the community.

— **Peter F. Drucker,**
"The Age of Social Transformation," *The Atlantic Monthly* (November 1994)

MEANING IN ACTION

The National Rifle Association (NRA) illustrates the vitality that emerges when members feel their organization has a larger purpose. NRA is a controversial organization that raises fierce passions among both detractors and proponents—which is indicative of the powerful sense of purpose it has developed and actively maintains.

For many members, participation in NRA offers more than programs and shooting competitions. They view membership as an opportunity to personally contribute to protecting the U.S. Constitution. The educational agenda of NRA embeds straightforward instruction in firearms safety and operation in the broader context of second amendment political issues. Even the selection of Charlton Heston as NRA president was done with an eye toward meaning. The association linked itself with the unique cultural symbolism of the actor's career.

HOW ENGAGING IS YOUR PURPOSE?

For purposes of this exercise, assume you have surveyed your members and staff about how they feel about your organization's purpose. You now have the survey results back, indicating their attitudes. Fill in the percentages reported for each category, distributing 100 percentage points across the choices below.

_____ Commitment. Fully responsible for achieving the purpose. Takes leadership in creating new opportunities.

_____ Enrollment. Freely chooses to be part of the purpose. Will work to achieve goals.

_____ Genuine compliance. Sees the benefits of the purpose. Does everything expected and more.

_____ Formal compliance. Does what is expected and no more.

_____ Grudging compliance. Does not see the benefits of the purpose and expresses doubts. Does just enough to maintain a position in the group.

_____ Noncompliance. Does not see the benefits of the purpose and will not do what's expected.

_____ Apathy. Neither for nor against the purpose. No interest. No energy.

Adapted from *The Fifth Discipline, The Art & Practice of the Learning Organization*, by Peter M. Senge (1990).

MEANING IN ACTION

The American Forest & Paper Association (AF&PA) looked to the future and intentionally elevated its sense of purpose. Growing pressures on forest resources had led to the emergence of a new concept of "sustainable forestry"—practices that could yield a sustained harvest of forest products well into the future. Leading schools of forestry, environmentalists, and a few companies were developing these ideas, but they were not widely understood or implemented in the industry. AF&PA's leaders concluded that the industry would eventually need to evolve in this direction.

In 1994 AF&PA created the Sustainable Forestry Initiative (SFI) Program. The association involved its members in a year-long process of developing environmental principles, objectives, and performance measures. It created an independent Expert Review Panel composed of 18 professionals from environmental organizations, universities, government, and industry to design a verification system. The Expert Review Panel initiated its own Forest Monitoring Project, managed by the Izaak Walton League of America, to assess how well the data reported by SFI program participants matched actual operations in the field. More than one-third of AF&PA member forestlands have either undergone or committed to an independent audit for certification under the SFI Standard.

Taking the association to a higher level of meaning, leadership, and environmental responsibility was not easy or without cost. When the association made conformance with the SFI Program a condition for AF&PA membership, a number of companies withdrew. Subsequently, 16 more members were expelled for failure to comply. But the association's willingness to uphold its goals at the cost of losing some members has improved the credibility of the entire forest products industry. New partnerships and working relationships are being built with government and public interest groups, including some of the industry's former strongest critics. The association's prestige and membership are at an all-time high.

3. Do we need to upgrade our sense of purpose or even re-purpose because changes in technology, the economy, or society are making our traditional purpose less relevant?

The acceleration of technological development, the emergence of an economy with new competitors, and the wide array of challenges facing society are fomenting change. In many cases, these developments are making traditional organizational purposes less relevant or even obsolete. In exploring your larger purpose, you may discover that you need to up the ante on your purpose, or even re-purpose your organization.

If you can connect your organization to an agenda for change that will both benefit your members and help deal with the problems and challenges facing society, you can ride the wave of the future. Not every association deals directly with a subject vital to the future, but every association can build connections to important challenges, such as maintaining a vibrant economy, protecting the environment, or promoting fairness in our society.

My most urgent message is that it is time for every person, every organization, and every nation to rethink their role…Everyone needs to be involved. Everyone has a role to play….

It is the bringing together of politics, science, business, religion, and morality that will provide the key to solving the problems that humankind is facing today. And it is the personal involvement of each individual that will allow a new civilization to flourish on earth.

— **Mikhail Gorbachev**
The Search for a New Beginning: Developing a New Civilization

In the mid-1990s, the American Public Transportation Association (APTA) involved innovative directors of transit systems around the country in a task force on Mobility for the 21st Century (M21). But M21 went far beyond looking at transit systems. Participants spent a year examining how problems related to current patterns of low-density urban sprawl could worsen, and they explored new ideas about patterns of urban development. The participants became advocates not just for better transit but also for better patterns of "smart growth," which give people new options of where to live and how to travel.

In 2001, APTA launched the Public Transportation Partnership for Tomorrow (PT)^2, the biggest education, outreach, and investment initiative in its history. (PT)^2 is designed to build support for public transportation among the public; opinion leaders; and local, state, and federal officials to positively influence funding decisions. The initiative will highlight the community benefits of expanding personal opportunity by providing everyone choice, access, and freedom of mobility. While directly serving the bottom-line interests of members, the campaign highlights the highest purpose of the industry: helping members be successful in improving American transportation.

Associations can evolve their purpose and still retain the fundamental essence that attracts their members. They can even outgrow their original purpose and remain successful. The classic example is the March of Dimes, founded in 1938 by President Franklin D. Roosevelt to find a cure for polio. The first campaign, which asked everyone to donate a dime, led to the foundation's name. Within 20 years, research funded by the March of Dimes led to the polio vaccine developed by Dr. Jonas Salk. Following this victory, the March of Dimes turned its attention to conquering birth defects. Today, the March of Dimes is one of the 10 largest voluntary health agencies in the United States, with 101 chapters nationwide. Its revised purpose gives volunteers the opportunity to continue helping America's children lead healthier lives.

4. *What do we know about the purpose(s) that would be most meaningful to potential members?* If your association involves only a segment of the people in the field you represent, what purposes might be most appealing to the segment you are currently not reaching? If your association includes members under age 30, the Millennial Generation may surge into your association within the next 10 years—if they find it attractive. How can you position your association to engage the Millennials, and what does that imply for your association's purpose? (See chapter 4, Generational Synergy, for more information.)

When we're talking about values and ethics we are essentially trying to answer two questions: Who are we? Who are we trying to become? Those are very esoteric for some folks, but the resulting discussions tend to be the most critical ones that evolve in strategic planning. They get to the very heart of all we do.

— Jeffrey Cufaude
Consultant, like minded people

All of these questions imply that your association has no fixed and final purpose. Instead, purpose evolves as association leaders and members create it together. An organizational structure that forces people to accept a purpose as given and unquestionable can stultify an association. Does your structure allow your members to find meaning together and keep the organization's sense of purpose vital and relevant?

Meaningful Relationships

Purpose alone is not enough to give meaning. People need relationships to feel valued, loved, wanted, and respected by others. As members in associations work together to achieve goals, they are developing caring and committed relationships. Even if they do not initially care deeply about one another, the process of working cooperatively for common goals creates an environment for friendship and shared purpose.

Associations have been using primarily low-tech ways to foster meaningful relationships. They publish member directories and provide networking opportunities at meetings. In the future, associations must accelerate the process of helping members move beyond the name, title, and affiliation on a name badge to making lasting connections with one another.

CREATING MORE MEANINGFUL RELATIONSHIPS

ATTRIBUTES	ACTIONS
Interaction	Pay attention to how the physical spaces you use promote or limit interaction. Create new formats for virtual interaction between members.
Belonging and Recognition	Develop new ways to give recognition and visibility to *all* members—even the newest ones—who make worthwhile contributions.
Friendship	Choose settings and activities that help members turn professional relationships into friendships of head and heart.
Deeper Bonds	Provide powerful experiential learning activities and opportunities for deeply meaningful dialogue for members who want deeper interactions.

Promoting interaction is the minimum requirement for helping people form relationships. The prevailing thinking in volunteer management is to offer people short-term opportunities to contribute something valuable to the association. But volunteers who work alone are less likely to create sustainable connections to the association. When volunteers are invited to work with one or more colleagues, relationships grow. These shared experiences build group cohesiveness, even as individuals re-form into new groups and projects.

In my experience, associations are never "value neutral." Whatever their scope, focus, or nature, they all start from a recognition that they are a subset of some larger population who share some common interest that is better addressed collectively. That sense of shared identity and purpose means there are dominant and common values, even if they are not explicitly articulated or even recognized.

— Mark Golden, CAE
Executive Director, National Court Reporters Association

Associations can emulate the way *Fast Company* has used shared experience to move beyond its origins as a business magazine. Its Company of Friends program allows local readers to get together, network, and discuss business issues. Participants of Company of Friends discussions no longer read the magazine solely to extract the information content. They now have the additional incentive to read the magazine so they can participate in the discussion groups. Providing forums for meaningful interaction enables *Fast Company* to deepen the loyalty of these readers and transform them from passive consumers of content to active participants in an ongoing dialogue.

TELLING STORIES

Every association's products and services are, knowingly or unknowingly, wrapped within stories that affect the hearts and minds of members. Think about your own association and answer the following questions.

What are the most meaningful stories, themes, and images that you identify with your association? What do your stories say about who you are? What values and actions are celebrated in the stories that are shared among your leaders and members?

What are the highest authentic aspirations that you and others in your field have for contributing to a better future? How can you touch on those aspirations in your stories, themes and images?

What emotional states and needs are common among different groups of your members? How can you make your stories and themes more responsive to the emotional needs of your members?

Stories must have symbolic integrity to effectively imbue meaning. That is, all parts of the story must reinforce, not detract from, the key messages. Think about your association's last major event. What were the prominent themes and symbols: Did they amplify or muffle your key messages?

It is possible to foster even deeper relationships and involvement in online environments, where people have never met face-to-face, by consciously creating community around the dynamics of recognition. Epinions.com, for example, is a Web site where individuals are encouraged to offer their opinions on just about anything. When readers agree with a reviewer, they can choose to "trust" that reviewer, which increases the reviewer's ranking.

This generates a friendly competition among reviewers to get increased recognition and have the meaningful experience of being a respected expert. Epinions illustrates a simple lesson: Feedback mechanisms that give participants recognition and visibility among their peers enhance the quality and quantity of participation.

To be more intentional about emotions, associations need to reflect on what different members need and what experiences they are having. Did the annual meeting evoke joy and pride? Did the board meeting appeal to petty interests or profound hopes? Does the staff feel vulnerable or valued? As studies of emotional intelligence have found, people who accurately perceive others' emotions are better able to respond flexibly to change and organize supportive social networks to achieve their goals. Likewise, associations that more accurately perceive their members' emotions can foster greater resiliency to respond to uncertain times.

Effective associations will extend meaningful relationships beyond the staff and members. Meaningful relationships can be found in the alliances that associations form and the coalitions they join. They turn supplier relationships from outsourcing agreements into true partnerships. A reliable predictor of an association's potential effectiveness in achieving its purpose is the extent of its healthy relationships with other organizations and institutions.

Meaningful Stories

When families or old friends get together, what do they do? They usually tell stories.

What are your association's favorite stories? The most powerful stories, themes, and images are not only captivating. They also are the carriers of your association's shared history and values. They communicate what your association is like and what it aspires to create.

Your leaders are your most important storytellers. They tell stories every time they interpret the actions of the association, whether in a board or staff meeting or at your annual meeting. Would these stories have more meaning if they spotlighted relationships rather than achievements? The association is not a monolithic "it." Specific individuals working together make things happen. If they have a role in your association's stories, you will soon have more heroes.

Remember that belonging is not a place; it is a state of mind and heart. For instance, volunteer recognition is an act of gratitude and appreciation that evokes pride and honor. Donations and sponsorships seldom work out as reciprocity; their value is in the emotions of generosity and recognition. Education fosters feelings of security and competence.

Associations have an essential function in providing social occasions that are conducive to making direct acquaintance. The shaping of members' social experience becomes essential. I'm a member of professional associations, and their meetings are little more than exercises in crowded anonymity. There may yet be much to be learned about how to shape meaningful, direct experience for members.

— **Ernest Sternberg, author of** *Economy of Icons*
   Guest Expert, ASAE Foundation Futures Scan Community of Practice

Meaningful Contribution

The creation of meaning involves offering people opportunities to make meaningful, tangible contributions to society. Feeling that we are heroes in stories that are "bigger than us" gives meaning to our lives. By extending a helpful hand to the wider community, associations can further their mission while providing their members with the opportunity to shape a better future for all.

SUSTAINING RELATIONSHIPS THROUGH MEMBER LIFE STAGES

The meaning your members seek and their emotional states change and evolve as they move through different life stages within your association. The chart below, developed by participants in a Futures Scan focus group, illustrates typical emotions members may experience. Use this list as a discussion-starter with focus groups of members in different life stages in your association. Ask how you can help create meaningful relationships throughout their membership experience.

LIFE STAGE	EMOTIONAL STATE	RESPONSIVE STRATEGIES
New Members	• Frustrated • Uncertain • Fearful • Lonely • Inept • Hopeful • Enthusiastic	• Interactive introductory events at meetings • Asking them what they want • Job banks • Career path programs • Fostering technical competence
Mid-Career	• Excited • Anxious • Challenged • Out of control	• Small, interactive roundtables • Access to technical resources • Mentoring programs • Fostering managerial competence
Older Mid-Career	• Proud • Enjoying • Plateaued • Burnt out	• New challenges • Opportunity to create a legacy • Elder status for education and mentoring • Informal networking • Fostering leadership competence
Seniors	• Longing for affirmation	• Continued contact with their peers • Special recognition

Imbedded in every association's purpose is a natural link to a meaningful contribution. It might be investing in critical knowledge to move an entire profession or industry forward on some essential national priority. It might be educating young people in the skills they will need to excel as adults in a profession. It might be as simple as using the association's organizational skills to rally volunteers across a shifting constellation of public service opportunities.

The Vinyl Siding Institute (VSI) has developed a unique relationship with Habitat for Humanity International (HFHI) that demonstrates a partnership founded on meaningful contributions. VSI is the trade association for manufacturers of vinyl siding and suppliers of raw materials, equipment, and services. Since 1995, the industry has donated more than $1.3 million in vinyl siding and accessories for the construction of Habitat homes. In one month alone, more than 70 volunteers from VSI member companies taught installation techniques to Habitat volunteers and worked side-by-side in the construction.

HFHI has hundreds of community-based programs that pool community labor and resources to build low-cost housing for families in need. Vinyl siding isn't a particularly glamorous industry, but VSI was able to take an elemental aspect of its product—shelter—and find a way to make that aspect work for the benefit of the wider world. Through its affiliation with HFHI, VSI moved its purpose beyond the narrow concerns of commerce and infused meaning by encouraging members to share in the noble purpose of creating affordable housing.

A powerful strategy for making meaningful contributions possible is to create projects that have a "multiplier effect" so participants can see how a small action in the present leads to greater positive changes down the road. The National Society of Professional Engineers (NSPE) is one of three founders of Mathcounts, a nationwide math coaching and competition program for middle school students. It makes math achievement as challenging, exciting, and prestigious as a school sport. About 17,000 volunteers, a majority of them NSPE members, introduce nearly 500,000 students to Mathcounts educational materials annually. NSPE members directly mentor students and organize annual chapter and state competitions that attract nearly 28,000 participants.

NSPE finds meaning in protecting public health and safety through engineering. Integral to the future of this purpose is equipping the next generation with the math skills required by the engineering and science professions. The Mathcounts Foundation tracks students who have competed in this program and found that a significant number of its current volunteers were once student participants. NSPE finds itself in the enviable position of both helping train future members as well as building greater public awareness of how engineers make a difference in society.

Meaning in all its forms—in purpose, relationships, and contributions—is central to the success of associations. The challenge is to take meaning seriously. It is an intangible quality that never seems as urgent as day-to-day operational concerns, yet meaning matters more than anything else.

Offering Opportunities for More Meaningful Contributions
A Discussion Exercise for Association Leaders

Instructions

Time Required: A minimum of 1 hour

Group Size: Discussion should be done in groups of 6 to 8. If your group is larger, break into smaller groups.

Facilitation and Recording: Ask each group to appoint a facilitator/recorder to move the discussion along, take notes, and make sure everyone has a chance to express his or her ideas.

Step 1: Brainstorm on Being an Exemplar of Your Mission *(15 minutes)*

> Brainstorm actions your association or your members could take to be exemplars of your mission. An association concerned with some aspect of healthcare, for example, could make sure its insurance coverage for members applies to that area. An association in the housing industry could apply best practices in the creation of healthy indoor environments to its own offices, then popularize these best practices by writing trade press articles about its own office improvements.

Step 2: Brainstorm on Creating Lasting Legacies *(15 minutes)*

> Brainstorm major contributions your association and its members could make to the greater social good that would:
> - Be consistent with your mission.
> - Build on your unique capacities.

Step 3: Build on Your Ideas *(20 minutes—or more)*

> Pick two (or more) of the ideas you have generated and work together to develop them further. Ask yourselves the following questions:
> - How could we make the results more tangible?
> - Is there a way to create a multiplier effect?
> - Have we dared to think BIG enough?

Step 4: Report Out (*10 minutes*)

If more than one small group was involved in this discussion, have the groups report their results to each other.

Step 5: Frame Your Audacious Goals *(Follow-up Discussion)*

At the next meeting, or if you have an additional hour, set big, audacious goals. Address member participation, the effect on your field, and public recognition.

Provocative Questions
For Association Executives and Leaders

Associations create meaning through meaningful purpose, meaningful relationships, and meaningful contributions. Associations with a clear sense of purpose gain an enormous advantage in differentiating their value for members. Meaningful relationships are cultivated through shared work, community cohesiveness, and attention to emotions. Meaningful contributions are tangible channels for purpose and relationships in action.

1. Meaning emerges from the self-interests of individual members. What gives meaning to individual members?

2. Associations need an over-arching meaning that bridges generations and interests. What unifying theme will touch the greatest number of your members now? For future generations of members?

3. Old purposes can become obsolete or less relevant. Is it time to clarify, update, or elevate your sense of purpose?

4. Associations of the future will accelerate the development of meaningful relationships. What strategies can you use to help new members develop the ties long-term volunteers have?

5. Emotions cannot be separated from deep human relationships. What emotions are your members experiencing? In which settings? Will they lead to sustained relationships?

6. Stories carry your association's shared history and aspirations for the future. What stories do your members tell about you? What stories do your leaders tell? What do your products and services say about you? What meaning are you communicating—and how?

7. A reliable predictor of an association's potential effectiveness is the extent of its healthy relationships with other organizations and institutions. Does your association have meaningful relationships with its strategic partners, business partners, and valued competitors?

8. Imbedded in every association's purpose is a natural link to a meaningful contribution. What contribution could your association choose that would be a manifestation of all that is right about it and contributes to a larger purpose for society?

9. The means to meaning are purpose, relationships, and contributions. How can these be used to differentiate your value to members?

10. Clear purpose, strong values, and meaningful relationships are enduring qualities that attract and retain members. Who is your association not getting as members that it should? What segments of your membership are eroding? What changes in your approach to meaning could attract and retain them?

Provocative Questions

For Business Partners

Business partners also gain an enormous advantage with customers by differentiating on the basis of meaning. They, too, can use the meaning of purpose, meaningful relationships, and meaningful contributions to connect with their customers.

1. Business partners draw their meaning from the self-interests of their owners, staff, and customers and clients. What over-arching purpose will touch the greatest number of these individuals?

2. Relationship marketing depends on knowing your customers or clients and sustaining relationships even in a highly mobile society. What strategies can you use to capitalize on new technologies and enduring human connections to create meaningful and profitable relationships?

3. Meaningful contributions are tangible channels for your purpose. In what way might your company contribute to a larger purpose for society?

4. Meaning can help you differentiate your value to customers and clients. How can you use purpose, relationships, and contributions to differentiate your value in your marketplace?

5. Businesses can create forums for meaningful interaction around their products and services. What activities could change your customers from passive consumers to active participants in an ongoing dialogue?

6. Stories that spotlight relationships have more meaning than simply talking about achievements. How can you tell your story through your relationships and successes of your clients and customers? How can you connect to their emotional experiences with your products?

7. People who accurately perceive others' emotions are better able to respond flexibly to changing demands. How can you increase your awareness and connection to client emotions?

8. Meaningful contributions are manifestations of all that is right about your company. What contribution could you make to society's larger purpose that also might be consistent with the purpose and priorities of your clients?

Recommended Resources

Bowling Alone, by Robert D. Putnam (Simon & Schuster, 2000). Provides statistical evidence of the erosion of American participation in civic groups and why it is critical to rebuild our social capital.

Joining Together, Group Theory and Group Skills, by David W. Johnson and Frank P. Johnson (Allyn & Bacon, 1997). A comprehensive scholarship of all aspects of organizational dynamics, from group dynamics to interdependence, from leadership to conflict resolution.

Man's Search for Meaning, by Viktor E. Frankl (Washington Square Press, 1984). Psychiatrist shares profound insights about meaning, clarified through his experiences as a Holocaust survivor.

On Leadership, by John W. Gardner (Free Press, 1993). Provides a brilliant, searching examination of leadership as it should be practiced in complex yet adaptive organizations.

The Search for a New Beginning: Developing a New Civilization, by Mikhail Gorbachev (Harpercollins, 1995). The former Soviet president turned futurist frames a new politics to rebuild society in this gem of a book-length essay. Availability may be limited.

Self-Renewal: The Individual and the Innovative Society, by John W. Gardner (W.W. Norton & Co., 1995). Leadership guru explores self-development, self-knowledge, the courage to fail, love, and motivation.

CHAPTER 2
Global + Local = Glocal

Glocalization: The growing synergy between globalization and localization that is creating an interdependent world.

G*localization* is not a misspelling of *globalization*. Rather, it's a term that characterizes how the processes of globalization and localization are going on at the same time. The interaction of these processes creates a more interdependent world.

Many decisions previously made at the national level are either moving upward to international organizations, devolving downward to state and local governments, or shifting sideways to nongovernmental organizations (NGOs), including associations. Local businesses increasingly market on a global scale, while global corporations practice "mass customization"— making their products and services more appealing to local markets. The very definition of "local community" is being altered with the proliferation of virtual communities.

International economics, politics, culture, and ethics are a dominant feature of our lives. In many arenas we focus on "harmonization" of policies and approaches across nations. However, these globalized features are interwoven by the growing need to understand and develop our local capabilities. The concept of "glocalization" reflects the increasing need to appreciate these contrasting dimensions and to operate on both planes.

— **Sherry Keramidas, Ph.D., CAE**
Executive Director, Regulatory Affairs Professionals Society

IMPLICATIONS FOR ASSOCIATIONS	ACTION STEPS
• The forums for representing members will change as national decision-making moves upward to international institutions, downward to state and local governments, and sideways to nongovernmental organizations.	• Determine where your association is focusing services now and what shifts would better represent and serve glocal members. What is the sustainable model for association structure within the new glocal context?
• Micro-enterprises will flourish in associations alongside multinational businesses.	• Glocal communities remove geographical boundaries. Which communities of interest in your association have this potential?
• Associations will play a growing role in harmonizing local and national standards with global standards.	• Think about what it means to be an association in a world that is a smaller, more intimate place in which to accomplish the "big things."
• The fusion of local cultures into a global metaculture forces people to resolve important questions about values and equity.	• Explore the interdependence of your organization on local chapters, international counterparts, and other partners and allies. Consider how new and evolving relationships will affect your organization.
• Communities of interest will form around topics, industries, and professions of every kind. These affiliations could shape personal identity more than nationality.	

All of these developments will increasingly glocalize the world of associations. In fact, associations have already experienced the effects of glocalization. Many associations focused on national issues have found their international membership and meeting attendance increasing. State-level associations and local chapters have found people from other countries popping up on their listserves or suggesting ideas for joint activities. Global standards are playing a larger role in shaping the competitive landscape in a wide variety of industries. Associations that built strong reputations as their members' "voice on Capitol Hill" are finding more of the political action shifting to state and local as well as international levels.

The full implications of glocalization are unknown. Yet it's clear that dealing with glocalization is likely to be a protracted, difficult, but ultimately rewarding process for associations. As glocalization develops, it will create new opportunities and generate new demands in at least four areas.

1.Decision Making

Glocalization is fundamentally altering the process of political decision making. A shift from national decision making upward to international institutions, downward to state and local governments, and sideways to private and nonprofit organizations is underway in earnest. This does not mean that nation-states are fading away. In fact, nationalism is flourishing in some areas where it was once suppressed by colonialism or Cold War politics. But, on the whole, a redistribution of decision-making roles is underway. National governments, to some extent, are losing their centrality.

The Shift Upward. Woodrow Wilson's concept of a League of Nations evolved 80 years later into an array of international economic, political, and military institutions. In fact, more than 5,900 international governmental organizations and networks exist. Many of them are quite influential in their own spheres of activity. For example, the World Trade Organization has a limited ability to override national legislation.

The United Nations once dealt only with governments. By now we know that peace and prosperity cannot be achieved without partnerships involving governments, international organizations, the business community, and civil society. In today's world, we depend on each other.

— Kofi Annan
Secretary General, United Nations

The international level has witnessed a growing influence of global corporate giants. Less known, but just as important, is the growing role of international associations and other NGOs in international governance processes. The Union of International Associations reports there are more than 38,000 international associations and NGOs. According to the Johns Hopkins University Comparative Nonprofit Sector Project, the NGO sector in 22 selected countries represents a $1.1 trillion industry. Based on these numbers, if the nonprofit sector were its own country, it would be the eighth largest economy in the world—ahead of Brazil, Russia, Spain, and Canada.

The International Chamber of Commerce (ICC) is an example of a nongovernmental representative body that speaks with authority on behalf of enterprises from all sectors in every part of the world. ICC promotes an open international trade and investment system and the market economy. Its conviction that trade is a powerful force for peace and prosperity dates from the organization's origins early in the 20th century. The small group of business leaders who founded ICC called themselves "the merchants of peace." Because its member companies and associations are themselves engaged in international business, ICC has unrivaled authority in making rules that govern the conduct of business across borders.

Although these rules are voluntary, they are observed in thousands of transactions every day and have become part of the fabric of international trade. The ICC World Council is the equivalent of the general assembly of a major intergovernmental organization. The delegates, however, are business executives, not government officials.

The Shift Sideways. Public–private partnerships and privatization movements illustrate how decision making can shift to the private sector. Indianapolis, Indiana, for example, mandates head-to-head competition between the public and private sector, creating competition with cost and performance criteria in the open marketplace. Government organizations, private businesses, and alliances of independent providers compete to provide services, such as airport management, waste collection, road maintenance, and printing.

The lines between public and private are blurring in the glocal world. Associations can help their members understand these changes and take advantage of the opportunities created. In virtually every area where public–private partnerships or privatization may be possible, associations already exist and can play a facilitating role.

GLOCALIZATION IN ACTION

The International Society for Prevention of Child Abuse and Neglect (ISPCAN) was initially founded as a professional society to provide child abuse prevention research and education for members from the medical, mental health, legal, and social welfare fields. As ISPCAN's membership expanded to 1,700 members from 100 countries, its leaders realized the organization was addressing issues and serving members primarily in the Western world.

True to its global mission, ISPCAN now offers more assistance to professionals in developing countries. Through peer nominations and scholarships, it provides complimentary memberships so members can participate in congresses and conferences worldwide. ISPCAN supports national and local training in developing countries and publishes and seeks information on global issues. It is local members, however, who design the programs, identify the priority issues, and teach others how to work within the local environments. ISPCAN offers the models, experiences, and research for local chapters to analyze and modify for their unique environments, cultures, religious, and socioeconomic situations.

Board members, who represent 16 countries, recognized ISPCAN could not tap the existing member dues as a revenue source to provide these global services. The society created a fundraising function and established itself as an NGO, working in partnership with the United Nations through UNICEF and the World Health Organization.

The Shift Downward. Decision making is also shifting downward to state and local levels. In the United States, this "new federalism" has been developing under both Democratic and Republican administrations. Power is devolving from the federal government to state and local governments on such issues as education, crime, and the environment. A similar phenomenon is occurring in most industrial nations. For associations, this trend will lead to greater investment in government affairs at the state and local level.

If I were head of a professional association or industry group, I would try to help my constituents expand their market share locally. I'd try to figure out if there were particular obstacles to my constituents competing effectively in their own backyard (such as the absence of health insurance for small businesses) and seek to mobilize appropriate-scale remedies (like pool insurance purchasing).

— Michael H. Shuman
Author, *Going Local: Creating Self-Reliant Communities in a Global Age*
Guest Expert in the ASAE Futures Scan Community of Practice

At the community level, movements are underway to promote goals as diverse as downtown revitalization, brownfields redevelopment, "smart growth," small business ownership, community sustainability, traditional neighborhood development, manufacturing, and agriculture. Some of these efforts may seem naïve in light of growing multinational corporations and the momentum of globalization. But proponents of local development argue that it actually benefits globalization by acting as a stabilizing force.

In a tightly interconnected global economy, where downturns anywhere can be contagious somewhere else, maintaining a vigorous local and regional economy can help communities keep some control over their future and make the whole global economy less vulnerable. As more association members look to local economies for their livelihood, they will shift their allegiance to associations active in local issues and relationships.

It used to be that when decisions were made on the local level, those decisions were often based on the immediate; in some cases little thought was given to how a dam upstream might cause lack of water downstream. Local decisions can affect the whole world. What is so exciting is the immediate access to a plethora of information for reaching a decision and/or gaining immediate feedback as to how one decision might affect other areas.

— Frances Shuping, CAE
Vice President, Tecnology and Communications, Air Condition Contractors of America

2. Marketplace

With advances in telecommunications and the reduction of tariffs and trade barriers, goods and services—and the currency to pay for them—flow ever more freely across borders and oceans. Web sites such as e-Bay and Walmart.com demonstrate how the local bazaar will be increasingly replicated in cyberspace.

Small businesses (under 20 employees) account for the majority of job growth in the United States. Micro-enterprises—businesses of fewer than five employees—are anticipated to provide the overwhelming majority of new job opportunities in the developing world. The Internet and relatively inexpensive global transportation are creating a world where Davids—small businesses and micro-enterprises—can flourish alongside multinational Goliaths in the world economy. A growing glocal segment of the marketplace will potentially create a new group of business owners in need of services provided by existing or new associations.

While small businesses are going global, transnational corporations are going local. Mass customization—the ability to produce large quantities of products that appeal to the unique characteristics of local or niche markets—is becoming the norm. Associations need to understand the principles of mass customization and the degree of localization that may be required for their product offerings to be more competitive in specific markets.

WHAT SHOULD YOU GLOCALIZE?

With staff, brainstorm what goods and services that your association currently provides could be glocalized in the future. How might you adapt products and services to reflect local cultural practices? For example, discuss whether your publications should have different versions for various regions or should be made available in multiple languages. You might want to consider having three regional meetings instead of one large national annual meeting.

Honda executives were among the first to talk about glocalization, using the term to describe their mass customization strategy for marketing the Honda Accord automobile. Honda made the Accord the world's best-selling automobile by creating assembly lines in eight different worldwide manufacturing plants. Each produced a slightly different model adapted to the preferences of local populations. An American Accord and the European model are 95 percent identical. It is the 5 percent variation (or localization) of the product that made it a best-seller.

GOAL: A POLIO-FREE WORLD

Rotary International is a worldwide organization of business and professional leaders who provide humanitarian service, encourage high ethical standards in all vocations, and help build goodwill and peace in the world. There are approximately 1.2 million Rotarians, members of more than 29,000 vibrant Rotary clubs in 161 countries.

Rotary is organized at club, district, and international levels to carry out its program of service around the globe. Rotarians are members of their clubs, and the clubs are members of the global association. Each club elects its own officers and board of directors and enjoys considerable autonomy within the framework of its constitution and the constitution and bylaws of Rotary International.

Throughout its history, Rotary International has collaborated with many civic and humanitarian organizations, as well as government agencies of various nations. An example of what these partnerships can accomplish can be found in Rotary's PolioPlus program. Launched in 1985 in concert with the World Health Organization, the U.S. Centers for Disease Control, and UNICEF, the program's goal is to immunize every child in the world against polio. By 2005, Rotary International will have committed nearly a half-billion U.S. dollars to the effort and sent millions of volunteers to assist in vaccine delivery; social mobilization; and logistical help at the local, national, regional, and international levels.

AID AROUND THE WORLD

The International Federation of Red Cross and Red Crescent Societies is the world's largest humanitarian organization. Founded in 1919, the federation comprises 176 member Red Cross and Red Crescent societies, a Secretariat in Geneva, and more than 60 delegations strategically located to support activities around the world. (The Red Crescent is used in place of the Red Cross in many Islamic countries.)

The federation carries out relief operations to assist victims of disasters, combined with development work to strengthen and support its member national societies. The federation's work focuses on four core areas: promoting humanitarian values, disaster response, disaster preparedness, and health and community care.

The unique network of national societies—which includes almost every country in the world—is the federation's principal strength. Cooperation between national societies gives the federation greater potential to develop capacities and assist those most in need. At a local level, a vibrant and active network enables the Federation to reach individual communities.

The Secretariat in Geneva coordinates and mobilizes relief assistance for international emergencies, promotes cooperation between national societies, and represents the national societies in the international arena. Field delegations assist and advise national societies with relief operations and development programs and encourage regional cooperation.

As the glocal marketplace develops, universally accepted approaches to issues such as labor rights and intellectual property must be developed. As an example, shortages of qualified software programmers prompted the United States to create special 6- to12-month "working visitor" visas (and led to some protests about "foreign workers taking American jobs").

Automobile manufacturing facilities just across the Texas–Mexico border spurred the debate about global wage equity and working conditions as well as environmental and health standards. Standards for intellectual property rights vary widely worldwide. Disputes over pharmaceutical patents, distribution of movies, and ownership of Web-based content are other examples of international controversies that need to be resolved for the glocal marketplace to mature. Associations can play a key role in fostering dialogue around differences in global standards on such topics through outreach efforts with collateral organizations in other countries.

3. Culture

In 2000, the world's number-one toy was Pokemon, a Japanese creation. The most-used condiment was Mexican salsa; the leader in cell phones was Nokia, a Finnish company; and the world's fastest growing franchise was Pizza Hut, which serves an American version of Italian food. A global metaculture containing a great deal of diversity already exists.

The Internet, global satellite television, and easy travel make it easier for consumer products—and ideas—to travel to all ends of the earth. The young Millennial generation is proving especially comfortable operating in this global metaculture. Teenagers around the world are wearing the same attire, listening to the same music, and speaking (or typing, in chat rooms) the same slang. Fusion cuisine restaurants incorporate various kinds of ethnic food into interesting combinations of flavors and recipes. Movies play simultaneously on three or four continents; local (national) television companies import stories, program ideas, and actors from other markets.

Although this emerging global metaculture contains local diversity, many fear it will eradicate the unique qualities of local cultures. Traditionalists are concerned that modern viewpoints will dislocate their long-held beliefs. What happens to local language, food, and customs as the influence of English, American fast food, and Internet culture grows? Intellectuals in nearly every country outside the United States are preoccupied with the question of how to avoid an

American-dominated global "monoculture" and evolve toward a "glocal culture"—one in which globalization proceeds without destroying the best qualities of the world's diverse local cultures.

For the cultures of the world to work together and for diversity to flourish, nations must agree on certain values and rules. But agreements of this kind are not fully in place. Compared to the U.S. economy, the world economy lacks sufficient common values or institutional arrangements to protect the weak and vulnerable. For instance, nations disagree on matters such as human rights, the acceptance or rejection of corruption, the need to limit environmental impacts, religious tolerance, and the importance of closing the gap between the haves and the have-nots.

In an increasingly borderless world, these types of disagreements need to be confronted and worked through. Because associations span every area of the economy and society, they can facilitate conversations about nearly all of the issues involved in creating a glocal culture that is both diverse and unified.

Trade associations, for example, might hold international discussions about eliminating bribery and corruption in global business practices and adopting environmentally advanced practices and technologies. Professional societies can discuss professional ethics and legitimate variations in standards and practices based on cultural differences.

4. Community

Geography is no longer the sole basis for creating community. Associations themselves represent a new form of community that has emerged as a result of advancing transportation and communication technologies. Now the Internet is breaking down the former barriers of time and distance.

A virtual community of interest may or may not meet face-to-face, have a formal organizational governance structure, or have a commonly held mission or purpose. What it *will* have is people bonded together around a common area of interest, regardless of gender, nationality, ethnicity, or education level. Even if its membership is global, it will be an intellectual home to the people involved—a glocal community.

Virtual community makes it possible to organize on a *multi-local* basis to create global change. For instance, scores of local forest protection groups around the world, linked by the Internet, have organized Global Forest Watch to monitor for illegal cutting or burning in old-

---

FOSTERING MULTI-LOCAL SYNERGY

To launch a major initiative designed to foster multi-local synergy:

- Identify organizations similar to your association in other countries.

- Foster counterpart relationships between local U.S. chapters and international local chapters having similar areas of interest, issues, and membership bases.

- Provide guidance and training to your local chapters on effective advocacy and coalition building with local chapters of other associations.

- Create global forums for interactions using listserve technology, Web sites, and chat sessions at meetings.

- Develop skills to deal with global management challenges, such as creating inclusive strategies for membership, programs, and communications.

---

growth forests. Another community of interest, focused on banning land mines, used e-mail and Web sites to link small local groups into a large global network to advance its cause; the group received a Nobel Peace Prize for its efforts. In the future, global multi-local activities will form around topics, industries, and professions of every kind as either informal *ad hoc* alliances or permanent associations.

Globalization suggests a future centered on huge organizations, economies of scale, and economic might. Localization suggests preservation or further development of local community, ownership, initiative, and control. Glocalization acknowledges positive aspects of both and asks—How can we make the world a "smaller," more intimate place in which to accomplish "the big things?"

As glocalization lessens the influence of nationality on people's lives, more people will use an affiliation or membership in a community of interest (or association) as a key component of their identity. In the future, association membership could become as important as nationality, ethnicity, alma mater, or hometown.

Provocative Questions
For Association Executives and Leaders

Glocalization is the process of globalization and localization interacting to create an interdependent world. National decision making is moving upward to international institutions, downward to state and local governments, and sideways to nongovernmental organizations. The Internet helps create a glocal marketplace in which any size business can operate both globally and locally. The emerging glocal culture should be both diverse and unified. Communities are forming around common interests without regard to geography.

1. Your association will need to change its services to represent and serve glocal members. What effect will the glocal marketplace have on the goods and services you provide? What will be your sustainable business model in this new context?

2. Glocal communities remove geographical boundaries. Which communities of interest in your association have this potential?

3. Your association operates in a world that is a smaller, more intimate place in which to accomplish "big things." What new possibilities are represented in this paradox for your association?

4. Many decisions previously made at the national level have shifted upward to international organizations, downward to state and local governments, or sideways to nongovernmental organizations, including associations. How will glocal decision-making change your role in advocacy?

5. Associations will play a growing role in harmonizing local and national standards with global standards. What new initiatives will be required to achieve global harmonization of important standards?

6. Maintaining some degree of local self-reliance can help communities keep some control over their futures and make the whole global economy less vulnerable. What leadership role, if any, should your association take in fostering this trend?

7. A unique marriage between local (small) businesses and global (large) markets will drive more commerce to the online world. Should your association facilitate this trend? What new tensions will this create for traditional business relationships?

8. Many people fear a global metaculture will soon eradicate the unique qualities of local cultures. What role can your association play in facilitating a glocal culture that honors local cultures and customs?

9. Critical issues for global peace include the have/have-not gap, the rights of women and children, sustainable development, and religious tolerance. What role could your association play in this global dialogue?

10. More people will use an affiliation or membership in a community of interest (or association) as a key component of their identity. What steps can your association take to help your members create an identity as a global citizen of an industry, profession, or cause?

Provocative Questions
For Business Partners

Glocalization is the process of globalization and localization interacting to create an interdependent world. Associations and their members are moving into new arenas, and they expect their business partners to keep pace. The glocal marketplace is strongly influencing the production of goods and services; "the rules" have changed for what is made, who is making it, and how it is marketed.

1. Your glocalness will be a selling advantage. Are you capable of operating globally and locally? What new capacities might you need?

2. Consider which of your products and services lend themselves to regional or local customization. Is there a sustainable business model to allow you to do this?

3. Local chapters and organizations may grow in influence and buying power. Do you have the presence to develop strong relationships with local buyers?

4. A glocal culture should not be a monoculture or an export of American culture. What changes should you make to honor the diversity of local cultures?

5. Your business may be far ahead of association clients in operating glocally. Can you lend your expertise and relationships to open doors for the association?

6. You may be an early detection system for important shifts in glocal decision making, because you operate in different circles than your association clients. Are you engaged in your association's public policy processes to alert it to new challenges?

Recommended Resources

ASAE Global Opportunities. An online resource to help ASAE members manage their association's transition into the global marketplace (www.asaenet.org/go).

Associations and the Global Marketplace: Profiles in Success, by Kimberly Svevo-Cianci (American Society of Association Executives, 1995). Includes case studies and smaller "snap shots" that illustrate the experiences of associations in meeting the challenges of entering the global marketplace.

A Future Perfect: The Challenge and Hidden Promise of Globalization, by John Micklethwait and Adrian Wooldridge (Times, 2000). Emphasizes the ways in which globalization can reduce restrictions on where people can go; what they can buy; where they can invest; and what they can read, hear, or see.

Global Civil Society: Dimensions for the Nonprofit Sector, by Lester Salamon, et al. (Johns Hopkins University, 1999). A systematically comparative and methodologically rigorous map of the economic dimensions of the nonprofit sector in 22 countries, from six different regions.

Globalization and the Challenges of the New Century: A Reader, by Patrick O'Meara and Howard D. Mehlinger (editors) (Indiana University Press, 2000). A collection of articles written by leading thinkers about globalization.

Going Global: An Association Primer, ASAE Background Kit (American Society of Association Executives, 2000). Examines the variables involved in evaluating, planning, and managing an international association program.

Going Local: Creating Self-Reliant Communities in a Global Age, by Michael H. Shuman (Free Press, 1998). Illustrates how several communities have resisted the encroachment of large multinational corporations by nurturing locally owned businesses.

Global Forum of Societies of Association Executives. A network for the professional association executive community worldwide (www.asaenet.org/globalforum).

The Lexus and the Olive Tree: Understanding Globalization, by Thomas Friedman (Anchor, 1999). An anecdotal and well-written account of the unfolding process of globalization, written by a *New York Times* foreign-affairs columnist.

CHAPTER 3
Inclusivity

Every nation contains varied subcultures and perspectives that people in the dominant culture find hard to see. Each nation has unique circumstances that have shaped the way different people think and act. These circumstances change over time. The populations of all the industrial nations, for example, were once much younger on average; they will become older still over the next 30 years. The perspectives in those countries are bound to differ from perspectives in developing nations, where rapid population growth is creating "youth cultures."

Inclusivity describes an approach to the whole range of differences in culture and personal perspectives that exist in every society and organization. It involves a heightened awareness of those differences, including knowing the limits of one's own viewpoints. Greater appreciation of the potential value of varied perspectives will lead to a fundamental shift away from assimilating differences to one that not only recognizes these differences, but celebrates and leverages them to achieve greater impact. Deliberate efforts will be made to use varied perspectives as a resource for innovating more powerfully, solving problems more effectively, and creating more stimulating environments.

Inclusivity is not about compassion. It is about good business strategy.

— Maria del Pilar Avila
Executive Vice President and Chief Staff Officer, New America Alliance

The roots of inclusivity extend from the perennial wisdom of the world's major religions to the philosophical outlook of postmodernism. In the

IMPLICATIONS FOR ASSOCIATIONS	ACTION STEPS
• Associations may unintentionally repress the variety of cultural and personal perspectives within them.	• Encourage staff and members to speak more from their unique perspectives.
• Associations will not thrive, perhaps not even survive, unless they are open to other cultural perspectives.	• Engage in dialogue with people having different cultural backgrounds and viewpoints
• The concept of inclusivity offers a new approach to differences in cultural and personal perspectives.	• Put yourself in situations where you are the cultural minority.
• Increasingly, differences will be valued and viewed as a resource for creative adaptation.	• Seek out books, movies, and other media that expose you to other cultural perspectives
	• Organize an inclusivity retreat.
	• Remain open to looking at your organization from several different perspectives

United States, one major source is the diversity movement. It originally arose to open the doors to the mainstream world of work for minorities and women but then kept expanding to embrace other forms of diversity.

Every association encompasses a variety of differences. Some relate to race, gender, and ethnicity. Others arise from factors such as age and generation, education, religious beliefs and values, sexual orientation, family status and stage of life, physical abilities and limitations, organizational positions, geographical location, military experience, learning and thinking styles, and personality. In addition, professions and areas of business often have their own mini-cultures.

Despite this variety of differing perspectives, associations sometimes assume that all members are the same. The rich tapestry of differences fades into the background as people are seen as fitting into one dominant culture or industry stereotype.

The resulting loss of creative variety could be a big disadvantage. The 2000 U.S. Census shows that Latino–American, Asian–American, African–American, Native American, and other ethnic groups jumped from 23 percent to 30 percent of the total U.S. population between 1990 and 2000. That statistic is merely a foretaste of what's to come. More than 40 percent of young Americans are minorities. As those young people grow up, they will contribute to the most dramatic demographic transition in U.S. history. During the coming decades, more than five-sixths of all new employees will be women and non-Euro-Americans. Demographers forecast that, by mid-century, America will have a "minority majority."

To thrive, or perhaps even to survive, associations have no choice but to be open to other cultural perspectives. Embracing inclusivity involves three major tasks: being aware of differences, valuing and preserving those differences, and synergizing differences.

Associations must recognize and embrace the unique qualities, cultures, and viewpoints of each employee, member, and stakeholder to enhance the overall effectiveness of the organizations.

— **Susan M. Darrow**
  Partner, Information Systems Consulting Group
  Chair, 2001 ASAE Diversity Committee

Being Aware of Differences

To include the richness of different cultures and personal perspectives in the work of associations requires an acknowledgment of their existence. Gaining this knowledge of others calls for a heightened self-awareness about the character of your own culture and the limits of your personal viewpoints.

Having little appreciation for another's culture, no matter how interesting or valuable it may be, is not a matter of malicious intent. It is much more subtle and much less intentional.

Typically, people in the dominant culture have a limited ability to see and appreciate the variety of perspectives that surround them. In particular, when we are part of a dominant culture we are usually unable to see *our own* cultural perspective as just one perspective among many. We don't even think of ourselves as *having* a culture. We assume our way of seeing things is simply normal—the way things are. Our inability to see ourselves as operating in a particular culture with particular limitations creates a subtle pressure on everyone else to conform. If they don't, we tend to see them as outsiders.

To become more aware of the variety of cultural and personal viewpoints in your association:

- Encourage staff members to view their unique perspectives (racial, ethnic, generational, values, and everything else) as potentially valuable for the association.

- Ask them to speak from those unique perspectives, bringing their "real selves" and their "office selves" closer together.

- Be a model yourself, by regularly engaging in serious dialogues with people with different cultural backgrounds or viewpoints. Set aside any desire to "win arguments" in favor of understanding the world from their points of view.

- Read books and watch movies that expose you to the cultural framework of minorities in your association, whether ethnic minorities or "opinion minorities."

- Put yourself in situations where *you* are the minority. For instance, spend time with your organization's techies, if you are a non-techie; go out with Generation X employees if you are a Baby Boomer, and so on.

- Organize an inclusivity retreat to explore the variety of cultural perspectives present in your association.

These activities can foster a greater self-awareness among people in your organization's dominant culture about what their culture is like, what its rules and priorities are, and how it may inhibit others. Only when you can see your own culture as one among many, with flaws as well as strengths, can you begin to see the creative variety of other cultures.

AN AWARENESS EXERCISE

Ask participants to complete the sentence "*I am a(n) _____.*" Tell them to fill in the blank with a word or phrase that describes something important about their identity or perspective.

Next, ask them to complete the statement in 10 different ways. Ask each person to place his or her list (written side down) on a table and pick up someone else's.

Debrief by calling out various categories and asking for examples from different lists. Here are some suggested categories:

- Age
- Gender
- Association membership
- A belief
- Marital status
- Ethnicity or tribe
- Family status
- Sexual orientation
- A value
- An interest
- Language spoken
- National origin
- Political party
- Organization
- Personal characteristic
- Personality type
- Political ideology
- A hobby
- Profession
- Specialty or professional approach
- Race
- Geographical region
- Religion
- Socioeconomic status
- Thinking style

Emphasize the main learning point that there are many more dimensions of difference than race or national origin.

A RAINBOW-HUED SOCIETY

Golfer Tiger Woods describes himself as Cablinasian, an amalgam of Caucasian, African American, and Native American from his father's side, and Asian from the side of his mother, a Thai partly of Chinese ancestry. Singer Mariah Carey proudly tells people she has a half-Venezuelan, half-African American father and an Irish mother.

Being multiracial—and being uniquely different—has a cachet. For the first time, respondents to the 2000 U.S. Census could choose more than one race to describe themselves. Nearly 7 million did just that. Intermarriage rates are soaring, and the numbers of multiracial children are growing accordingly. By 2050, 21 percent of Americans will be claiming mixed ancestry, according to projections by demographers Jeffrey Passel of the Urban Institute and Barry Edmonston of Portland State University.

Most Americans view a multiracial future optimistically. In a USA TODAY/CNN/Gallup Poll, 64 percent said it would be "good for the country" to have more Americans "think of themselves as multiracial rather than as belonging to a single race." Although only 47 percent of people over 65 hold this view, 74 percent of people 18 to 29 believe a multiracial future is good, so this outlook is almost certain to grow.

Valuing and Preserving Differences

The metaphor of the melting pot captures the 20th century American ideal of assimilation. People of every nationality, race, and ethnic group came to the United States and made it their home. This diversity created conflicts. But, as the differences melted away over the generations, everyone would eventually become simply an American.

The idea of the melting pot captured part of the American experience, but it never fully squared with reality. If it had, differences between ethnic and racial groups would not exist.

One area of life where the melting pot metaphor has held true for a long time is the workplace. Success in business has demanded conformity. Even in associations, staff members have tended to voluntarily abandon most of their ethnic distinctions while inside the office or attending meetings and conferences.

At the dawn of the 21st century, however, the melting pot is not an apt metaphor for describing American culture. As dramatic evidence of the change U.S. society has experienced, consider that immigrants, or even first-generation Americans, don't necessarily need to learn English to function and thrive. In the past, immigrants who left home were "gone for good." Today, with global telecommunications and travel, the reinforcement of home values is just a phone call away.

People now tend to be less apologetic about their cultural differences. Many, in fact, enjoy rediscovering their cultural roots; others try to preserve the best of their cultures. Still others are learning to delight in cultural diversity. The 2000 census figures show a large increase in the number of people who identify themselves as multi-racial or multi-ethnic and reject conventional demographic categories.

The melting pot metaphor suggested that mainstream American culture stayed fixed: All newcomers and minorities changed to fit into it. Today, however, a process of mutual adaptation is underway. The mainstream culture is itself in flux, as it accommodates the diversity mixture and a growing desire to maintain much of that variety. Cultural fusion—new forms of food, entertainment, business practices, and worldviews—will emerge as multiple cultures intersect.

This change in the larger society requires a parallel change in the association workplace, in the interactions of members, and in the association community as a whole. The goal is not to assimilate cultural differences into a dominant culture but to create a new heterogeneous culture that preserves potentially valuable differences. Shaking off the limits of a single dominant culture will allow associations to draw on a rich mix of perceptions and thinking to become more aware, flexible, and creative.

Synergizing Differences

How do you capitalize on internal variety while resisting fragmentation? How can you use differences in viewpoints to help solve problems more creatively, to avoid "groupthink," and to develop higher capabilities than more homogeneous groups can achieve? In general, the answers involve having a clear common purpose and creating an environment where people truly respect and support each other and continuously strive to understand each other better.

To explore the idea of synergizing differences, look at specific examples. For instance, the following chapter on Generational Synergy explores possibilities for fostering interaction between people of different ages. The same approach could apply to people of different ethnic or cultural backgrounds.

> **NAME BADGE EXERCISE**
>
> At your next meeting, instead of preprinting the usual name badges with title and organization, have people create their own. Ask people to write something on their name badge that makes them unique from every other person at the meeting.

THE PAYOFFS

Here is a sampling of the payoffs that accompany efforts aimed to diversity and inclusivity:

- Nancy Adler's research on synergy in work teams showed that only teams with varied backgrounds and outlooks were able to achieve the highest levels of synergy and performance. A. S. Tsui and L. W. Porter found in a study of work force diversity in 55 Orange County companies that good diversity management is a major factor in attracting and retaining qualified employees.

- The bipartisan Federal Glass Ceiling Commission cited statistics demonstrating that companies that were most successful in removing their "glass ceilings" saved millions of dollars on turnover costs. In addition, they earned twice the rate of return on investment as those that failed to deal well with diversity issues.

- Ann Morrison found that good diversity management correlates strongly with global competitiveness in U.S. companies.

- Rosabeth Moss Kanter demonstrated that companies with progressive human resource management—including affirmative action—enjoyed significantly greater profitability than average over a 20-year period.

- Robert Hayles ranked the 10 best companies in the food industry in terms of "diversity excellence" by comparing diversity training efforts, numbers of women and people of color, and a variety of other measures. The food companies ranked highest in diversity excellence were also the best financial performers over one-, five-, and ten-year periods.

- The Center for Creative Leadership identified 12 companies that showed exceptional leadership in encouraging diversity. All were in the top half of *Fortune* magazine's "most admired" companies, and 10 were in the top 20 percent.

No Boundaries

Inclusivity is a process with no clear end—only expanding opportunities. Perhaps *A Peacock in the Land of Penguins* says it best. The book tells a fable about birds of different feathers that left the chilly organizational climate of the Land of Penguins for the Land of Opportunity.

> "They came to realize that the Land of Opportunity is more than a place… It is a state of mind. The Land of Opportunity is

an attitude. It is openness to new ideas, a willingness to listen, an eagerness to learn, a desire to grow, and the flexibility to change.

"The Land of Opportunity is a new way of dealing with one another. It becomes a reality when we stop judging each other by superficial criteria and begin to see and appreciate everyone as uniquely talented, capable, and valuable.

"The Land of Opportunity is where we live and work when we choose to see with new eyes, live from our hearts, and allow ourselves and others to be what we truly are...ourselves."

INCLUSIVITY IN ACTION

In 1992 a study conducted by the American College of Healthcare Executives (ACHE) and the National Association of Health Services Executives (NAHSE) revealed that minorities represented more than 20 percent of hospital employees but held less than 1 percent of top-level management positions. It also disclosed that minority healthcare executives, with similar education and experience, still made less money, held lower positions, and had less job satisfaction than their majority counterparts. A follow-up study, conducted in 1997, included Hispanics and Asians. Although the gap had narrowed in some areas, differences remained.

The study prompted three healthcare organizations—the American Hospital Association, ACHE, and NAHSE to create the Institute for Diversity in Health Management. The Institute has recently gained a new partner, the Association of Hispanic Healthcare Executives. Since the institute's inception, many hospitals, national health care organizations, hospital alliances, health care systems, universities, and state associations across the country have become enthusiastic participants in it.

The Institute for Diversity in Health Management, a nonprofit organization, collaborates with educators and health services organizations to expand leadership opportunities to ethnic minorities. Its mission is to increase the number of ethnic minorities in health services administration and to improve opportunities for professionals already in the healthcare field. The Institute has designed several initiatives, including educational programs, a summer enrichment internship, professional development ,and leadership conferences.

More than 500 students have benefited from its Summer Enrichment Program. As part of its Educational Assistance Program, the Institute has awarded more than $110,000 in scholarships to promising undergraduate and graduate students. It has also placed nearly 20 advanced careerists in residencies and fellowships at healthcare organizations across the country.

The annual leadership conference is designed for trustees, senior executives, human resource officers, corporate diversity specialists, and other leaders who need to know how to articulate the business case for diversity. In addition, the institute developed a searchable Web-based database (DiversityConnection.org™) to provide job candidates and healthcare organizations another way to reach one another.

Inclusivity is too often misinterpreted as superficial representation, when in reality, it requires widespread infusion.

— Lorraine Cole, Ph.D.
Executive Director, National Black Womens Health Project

ARE YOU A CULTURAL CREATIVE?

Sociologists Paul Ray and Sherry Ruth Anderson have conducted surveys and focus groups to place the U.S. population into useful "psychographic" categories that reflect differences in values and lifestyles. They identify 26 percent of the U.S. adult population as Cultural Creatives. They believe many of these people are in associations because they are America's leading volunteers: More than 75 percent of them are involved in volunteer activities. However, they are minorities in most associations; like most minorities, they have simply tried to fit in the dominant culture.

By appealing to the Cultural Creatives who are already a part of their membership, associations might be able to explore new realms of creativity. This checklist can help you identify characteristics of a Cultural Creative. Check the boxes of statements you agree with.

- ○ I love nature and am deeply concerned about its destruction.
- ○ I am aware of the problems of the whole planet (global warming, destruction of rainforests, overpopulation, lack of ecological sustainability, exploitation of people in poorer countries) and want to see more action on them, such as limiting economic growth.
- ○ I would pay more taxes or pay more for consumer goods if I knew the money would go to clean up the environment and to stop global warming.
- ○ I place a great deal of importance on developing and maintaining relationships.
- ○ I value helping other people and bringing out their unique gifts.
- ○ I volunteer for one or more good causes.
- ○ I care intensely about both psychological and spiritual development.
- ○ I see spirituality or religion as important in my life but am concerned about the role of the Religious Right in politics.
- ○ I want more equality for women at work and more women leaders in business and politics.
- ○ I am concerned about violence and abuse of women and children around the world.
- ○ I want our politics and government spending to put more emphasis on children's education and well-being, on rebuilding our neighborhoods and communities, and on creating an ecologically sustainable future.
- ○ I am unhappy with both the Left and the Right in politics and want to find a new way that is not in the "mushy middle."
- ○ I tend to be somewhat optimistic about our future and distrust the cynical and pessimistic view given by the media.
- ○ I want to be involved in creating a new and better way of life in our country.
- ○ I am concerned about what big corporations are doing in the name of making more profits: downsizing, creating environmental problems, and exploiting poorer countries.
- ○ I have my finances and spending under control and am not concerned about overspending.
- ○ I dislike the emphasis in modern culture on success and "making it," on getting and spending, on wealth and luxury goods.
- ○ I like people and places that are exotic and foreign and like experiencing and learning about other ways of life.

If you agreed with 10 or more statements, you probably are a Cultural Creative; a higher score increases the odds.

Provocative Questions
For Association Executives and Leaders

Inclusivity acknowledges the existence of different cultures and perspectives, including a heightened self-awareness of the limits of one's own viewpoints. Preserving valuable differences will become a new priority. Differences in perspective will increasingly be viewed as a resource to help solve problems more creatively, avoid "groupthink," and develop higher capabilities than homogeneous groups can achieve.

1. Given the demographic snapshot from the U.S. Census 2000, what do you know about the changing demographics in your association?

2. A first step toward inclusivity is increasing awareness among people in your organization's dominant culture. What is the dominant culture in your association? How does it benefit you? How does it limit you? What are its rules and priorities?

3. Shaking off the limits of a single dominant culture allows associations to draw on a rich mix of perceptions and thinking to become more aware, flexible, and creative. How can your association create a culture that invites people to share their full selves with the organization? What activities will help people value different perspectives and experiences?

4. Associations may contain a significant number of members in a psychographic category called *Cultural Creatives*. Where are the Cultural Creatives in your association? How can you connect their potential to one another and to the association?

5. Do you have a diversity committee? How does your diversity committee define diversity?

6. What is the true mission of your diversity committee?

7. In what ways is your leadership reflective of your general membership?

8. Do the images in your communications and marketing materials reflect inclusivity?

9. Embracing inclusivity involves three major tasks: being aware of differences, valuing and preserving those differences, and synergizing differences. How can you infuse these concepts in all of your products and services?

Provocative Questions
For Business Partners

Business partners may experience inclusivity in much the same way associations do. Some may have greater opportunities to experience and build on the differences among people. They may be quicker to recognize the business imperative in inclusivity and be in a position to help associations discover the synergy of differences.

1. Given the demographic snapshot from the U.S. Census 2000, what do you know about the changing demographics in your organization?

2. Examine the dominant culture in your business. Is it suppressing differences and limiting your potential success in business? To whom do your products and services appeal? What would be gained if you could expand the range? What might be lost?

3. Products, services, and facilities should be universally designed with features that expand access. Features designed for one group often find broader appeal. For example, once decoder chips, sold primarily to people with hearing impairment, were required in all televisions, the primary user group shifted to people in loud environments like bars, in areas with multiple televisions, and to those learning English. What unexpected benefits have you discovered in stretching your business to be more inclusive?

4. How can you customize your products and services to help associations foster a greater sense of awareness?

5. How can you help your leaders and staff to understand and appreciate the cultural richness of associations?

Recommended Resources

Building a House for Diversity: How a Fable About a Giraffe & an Elephant Offers New Strategies for Today's Workforce, by R. Roosevelt Thomas, Jr., and Marjorie I. Woodruff (Amacom, 1999). Builds off a vivid metaphor for the difficult issues inherent in diversity to demonstrate how managing diversity can be seen as a set of skills that anyone can learn and use.

The Diversity Directive: Why Some Initiatives Fail & What to Do About It, by Robert Hayles and Armida Mendez Russell (McGraw-Hill, 1997). Includes a step-by-step process for initiating or revitalizing corporate diversity efforts, as well as case studies of successful diversity efforts that have been carried out in leading-edge companies.

Diversity Success Strategies, by Norma Carr-Ruffino (Butterworth-Heinemann, 1999). Offers insight into the moral and cultural forces that inform our most fundamental values and attitudes.

Implementing Diversity, by Marilyn Loden (McGraw-Hill, 1996). This guide provides successful strategies and tactics used by organizations committed to implementing diversity from the top down.

A Peacock in the Land of Penguins: A Tale of Diversity and Discovery, by Barbara Hateley and Warren H. Schmidt (Berrett-Koehler, 1997). Presents the complex issue of diversity in a simple and nonthreatening manner, through the use of an imaginative fable.

Redefining Diversity, by R. Roosevelt Thomas, Jr. (Amacom, 1996). Uses a new diversity paradigm to expand the concept of diversity beyond groups of people to include ideas and procedures.

CHAPTER 4
Generational Synergy

Generational synergy: different generations within an organization appreciate one another's virtues, support one another, and creatively interact.

Throughout history, the intersection of cultures has produced the periods of greatest creativity, such as when the writings of ancient Greece and Rome came to the forefront again in Medieval Europe and helped catalyze the Renaissance. Only when you actually engage yourself in a specific culture—interacting with its people, walking through its communities—do you experience its nuances. What was once a flat characterization, a stereotype, becomes a rich and complex terrain with unique qualities and merits.

It is the same with generations: The potential for maximum creativity often lies at their points of intersection. Associations bring multiple generations into contact with one another as members and staff. Yet confusion may result when a person from one generation behaves in a way that does not make sense to someone from another generation. That confusion can progress into biases that obscure the complexity—and the virtues—of a different generational outlook. In other words, talent is wasted, opportunities are squandered.

A better understanding of the outlooks of different generations within your association is necessary for bringing them into creative interaction. Every generation is forged in the fires of its experiences. Each generation has had vastly different life experiences; each also has distinctive contributions to make and roles it can play to support other generations.

IMPLICATIONS FOR ASSOCIATIONS	ACTION STEPS
• Associations flourish when all four generations feel welcomed and valued for their unique contributions.	• Ask Silents to stay involved in flexible capacities. Have them champion Generation X-ers in associations dominated by Boomers. Their job is to facilitate and be mentors for generational interaction.
• If you understand your own generation better, you can build connections from your experience to those of individuals in other generations.	• Ask Baby Boomers to create an association environment that appeals to the Millennial Generation. Help them move past Gen X stereotypes so they can work with younger people to build worthwhile legacies. Their job is to open doors and make way for younger generations to show what they can accomplish as leaders.
• Each generation has a lasting contribution to make to your association.	
• The upcoming Millennial Generation has low cynicism, high self-confidence, technical savvy, a strong achievement orientation, and a tendency to "associate" and work together as teams. They promise to become the greatest institution builders since the GI Generation. They could rejuvenate associations.	• Ask Generation X to provide hands-on, get-it-done leadership. Follow their lead on diversity. Help them move past Boomer stereotypes. Their job is to cut to the core of issues and take risks.

Generational synergy creates a great opportunity for associations to respect tradition while looking with creative optimism into the future.

— **Thomas C. Dolan, Ph.D., FACHE, CAE**
President and CEO, American College of Healthcare Executives

To foster synergy among generations, associations must invite individuals to play off of each other in a way that takes advantage of their different life experiences, outlooks, strengths, and skills. Generational synergy taps into the distinctive identity of each generation in accomplishing the association's purpose.

Understanding the Pattern of Generations

Most associations bring together people in all stages of their careers, in several age groups. To work together effectively, each age group needs to know about the life experiences, outlooks, and motivations of the other generations with which it interacts.

Generational characteristics differ around the world because people of the same age have divergent experiences living in different nations and cultures. Some economies may be in deep depressions while others are prospering; some nations may be at war, while others are experiencing religious revivals.

An association must understand the specific generational patterns of the nation or nations in which it operates. The United States, Canada, Australia, and parts of Western Europe have strong parallels in generational experiences and characteristics. In Eastern Europe, Russia, Asia, Africa, and much of Latin America, however, generational patterns are completely different. (The generational descriptions that follow apply to

Four Generations (adapted from *Beyond Generation X* by Claire Raines)				
	Silents	**Boomers**	**X-ers**	**Millennials**
Outlook	preservationist	idealistic	skeptical	optimistic
Work Ethic	dedicated	driven	balanced	energetic
View of Authority	reverent	love/hate	unimpressed	respectful
Leadership by	hierarchy	consensus	competence	achievement
Perspective	civic-minded	team-oriented	self-reliant	global

the United States. For discussions of generational characteristics in other nations and cultures, see the "Beyond America" online forum at www.fourthturning.com/cgibin/netforum/beyondamerica/a.cgi/1.)

The generational pattern in U.S. associations today includes three main generations: the Silent Generation (born between 1925 and 1942), the Baby Boom Generation (born between 1943 and 1960), and Generation X (born between 1961 and 1981). The once-dominant GI Generation (born between 1901 and 1924) has almost left the scene completely; the Millennial Generation (born after 1981) will begin to enter the workplace in large numbers.

Such generational labels are inevitably oversimplifications. Each generation could be broken into many subgroups. Even the labels and the years to define them vary from analysis to analysis. People born on the cusp of two generations often are a blend of the experiences in both. In addition, more affluent parts of each generation have different life experiences from those living in poverty. Nevertheless, generational labels can serve as a starting point for facilitating communication.

The Silent Generation (born 1925–1942)

After victory in World War II in 1945, a spirit of camaraderie pervaded American life. The GI Generation that won the war emerged with a "can do" attitude and sense of confidence that made them leaders and institution-builders. They ushered in an expansive postwar era characterized by material affluence, global power, and civic planning. From Dwight Eisenhower to George Bush, the GI Generation produced more U.S. presidents than any other generation.

The Silent Generation that followed shared their spirit of camaraderie, commitment to a common good, and sense of duty of the postwar era. But Silents found themselves overshadowed by the GI Generation before them, then overshadowed by the postwar Baby Boomers who followed.

Sandwiched between the two dominant generations of GIs and Boomers, Silents often developed strong negotiation skills. The Silent Generation produced many of the 20th century's greatest legislators. Their distinctive leadership role has often involved fine-tuning the institutional order and negotiating between the larger generations around them. They have excelled at bringing people together and modifying the extremes on either side of divisive controversies. The flexible, consensus-building leadership of Silents opened many of the paths that Boomers then went down.

Silents have led the way down a number of paths that are usually more associated with Boomers. The Silent Generation produced virtually every major figure in the modern civil rights movement. It accounted for the 1960s increase in helping professions like teaching, medicine, and the ministry, as well as the 1970s surge in "public interest" advocacy groups. Silents saw women entering the workplace during the war. New women entrants nearly disappeared from many fields during the 1950s, but two decades later Silent women came thundering back, accounting for nearly all of the nation's leading feminists.

In economic terms, Silents have had the fastest rising path of any generation for which income data are available. Born mostly during an era of depression and war, they experienced high unemployment, rationing, and low wages in their younger years. But from age 20 to 40, Silents showed this century's steepest rise in per-household wealth as their Depression-bred habits of frugality and saving paid off during the postwar boom. They became accustomed to government intervention, witnessing the birth of the War Production Board (WPA), and new government programs from Social Security to Medicare.

The Baby Boom Generation (born 1943–1960)

The baby boom after World War II gave rise to the largest generation in American history, one destined to be influential if for no other reason than its sheer size of more than 76 million. Boomers grew up during a time of historically unprecedented prosperity, indulged by their parents, and free from the financial fears and other major threats that characterized their parents' lives. The earlier cohort of the Boomer generation, in particular, saw what seemed to be a world of opportunity and worried little about the economic future. The question and ever-present danger in the lives of young Boomers was the cold war and the threat of nuclear war.

Advertising campaigns targeted to them heightened Boomers' generational self-awareness. As the first generation to grow up with television, and with so much attention focused on them, many Boomers felt part of a new American "youth culture," complete with its own music and heroes. They sometimes developed a self-preoccupation and sense of entitlement that set them apart from other generations.

The social movements for civil rights, women's rights, ecology, and other causes took place during the formative years of many Boomers. These created a sense of social idealism and a romantic individualism that valued creative individuality over institutions and favored questioning authority over conformity. Other Boomers went in a very different direction, toward evangelical religion and the political Right, but they, too, had a sense of idealism. A growing emphasis on throwing off constraints of the past and "doing your own thing" fostered creative experimentation; it also led to a weakening of the sense of duty that characterized the GI and Silent generations. While Boomers divided over the Vietnam War, the conflict prompted many to distrust the previous generations' belief that large institutions are the best way to solve problems.

The coming-of-age passions of the Boomer Generation calmed as its members took on jobs, raised families, and pursued the material comforts of an affluent society. Now many Boomers are dealing with both their aging parents and children of all ages, from older X-ers to budding Millennials. Older Boomers are moving toward their career peaks. People who, in their youth, flaunted their individualism and challenged America's institutions now spend much of their time in consensus-oriented meetings; they manage the institutions against which they once rebelled.

"I am a part of all that I have met."
— Lord Alfred Tennyson

Generation X (born 1961–1981)

Generation X is a highly diverse generation: One in three belongs to an ethnic minority, compared to one in four in the total population. X-ers grew up in the full swing of U.S. consumer culture and watched their parents work long hours to pay off homes. They, on the other hand, encountered a different world, one in which college graduates may carry a heavy debt burden and where single-family homes are often difficult to afford. Because the world didn't present to X-ers what they initially expected, they can be reluctant to commit. Skepticism is often their defense mechanism.

Much smaller in number than their predecessors, X-ers are also described as the Baby Bust generation. The sheer numbers and cultural dominance of Boomers can be disheartening to a small generation trying to stake out its own identity. X-ers tend to see Boomers as narcissistic and blind to their own faults. They are skeptical of whether Boomers will make the necessary sacrifices for the common good, such as ensuring Social Security and Medicare will support them in their old age.

Some X-ers have emerged as the hard-driving entrepreneurs behind the development of high-tech companies. But having experienced the consequences of their Boomer parents' hectic work lives, many X-ers intentionally seek balance, looking for flexible jobs with tangible outcomes that leave them time to "have a life." They tend to be unimpressed by titles, do not look for approval, and hence are, as other generations might say, "too comfortable with authority." This capacity frees them to voice fresh ideas without pretense.

MEET THE MILLENNIALS

Proactive efforts to understand and appeal to the Millennial Generation that will enter the workplace in the later '00s could pay off for associations. It is the biggest generation yet—even bigger than the Boomers. Imagine a huge, unstoppable mass hurtling down the track at you, a cadre of people so cohesive, directional, and energetic that their arrival is sure to transform you—unless they just decide to go around you.

Here's what Millennials are like, at this point in their lives, based on the Futures Scan's online discussions with William Strauss, co-author of *Millennials Rising*.

Sheltered—Millennials grew up in the era of child-proof cabinets, tamper-resistant packaging, safety features on every device, and constant supervision from adults. At every step of the way, protective Boomer and Gen X parents have ensured that their children could grow up with a minimal chance of being harmed. This sheltering process may have enhanced their basic idealism about the world, but it has left Millennials unaccustomed to threatening environments and hardship.

Confident—Millennials grew up during the "Long Boom." With the exception of the minor recession in the early 90's, and the slowdown in 2001, the American economy has been expanding rapidly since 1982. Millennials remember a decaying Russia, not the Soviet Union, and have grown up in a world where the global hegemony of America is unquestioned.

Group Oriented—Millennials were educated using group-teaching formats and socialized online with friends. It's no coincidence that "soccer moms" came on the scene while ferrying their Millennial kids to soccer practices. Millennials tend to develop strong team instincts and deep peer bonds; a cooperative sport like soccer is a perfect match for the Millennial mentality.

Special—The 1990s saw the emergence of *kinderpolitics*—the idea that the fundamental goal of social policy is to improve life for children. Proposals like the V-chip, the Family Medical Leave Act, and child tax credits all were enacted into law with the premise that it would be good "for the children." Millennials have been influenced by the constant concern for their welfare and believe, on some level, that they will play a special role in the future.

Achieving—Millennials have been held to high standards and strict accountability while growing up. Their experiences of youth include rigid zero-tolerance policies with severe punishments for minor infractions. In the classroom, their performance has been measured by a wave of higher school standards and standardized tests. Time analysis studies done at the University of Michigan's Institute for Social Research show that between 1981 and 1997 the amount of time that children age 3 to 12 spent studying increased by 20 percent.

Pressured—Millennials grew up with time pressures that have traditionally been faced only by adults. They have had to juggle the demands of homework, enrichment activities, hobbies, friends, and jobs. Pressure and time constraints seem perfectly normal for Millennials, which should allow them to thrive in fast-paced workplaces.

Conventional—Millennials find it natural to uphold social rules and standards that they feel are for the greater good. Millennial children nagged their parents to quit smoking and pestered their families to begin recycling. Millennials generally accept the basic values of their Boomer and X-er parents and are willing to work to uphold and even extend these basic standards. When students age 12 to 19 were asked by Roper Starch Worldwide in 1998 to rank the major problems facing America, the top five concerns were: selfishness, people who don't respect law and the authorities, wrongdoing by politicians, lack of parental discipline, and courts that care too much about criminals' rights.

What do we know about the Millennials? What do we have to offer them?

— **Richard B. Green**
Vice President Industry Relations and Association Sales, Marriott International, Inc.

The Millennial Generation (born 1982–to be determined)

The oldest Millennials are now making their presence felt on college campuses; by the later '00s they will be entering the association world. Even more so than the X-ers, diversity is the norm for Millennials—in 1997, for example, 37 percent of kindergartners were nonwhite.

What the Millennial generation will eventually be like—especially its younger members—is still an open question. They have grown up in an era of unprecedented prosperity, but their outlooks could change if the years ahead bring harder times or worsening social and environmental problems. Just as Boomers changed between grade school and their college years, and from when they entered the workforce to today, Millennials are sure to change as they go through life's stages.

If for no other reason than the sheer size of this cohort, it's likely that distinctive subgroups of Millennials will emerge, each of which may have its own personality.

At this point, however, middle-class Millennials have a distinctive character that could hardly be more different from the way that Boomers and X-ers were at the same age. Instead of questioning authority, Millennials tend to be rule followers who defer to authority. Instead of being skeptical and cynical, Millennials are optimistic and earnest. Rather than valuing nonconformity, they tend to be cooperative team players who speak almost apologetically when venturing opinions that depart significantly from the group norm.

Instead of seeking more personal time to "have a life," Millennials are used to full-time scheduled activity and hard work. Rather than "doing their own thing," they have grown up leading the most highly structured and supervised lives of any generation in living memory.

With low cynicism, high self-confidence, technical savvy, a strong achievement orientation, and a tendency to "associate" and work together as teams, Millennials promise to become the greatest institution builders since the GI Generation. They could rejuvenate associations—if Millennials find association involvement attractive. That depends on what the association community is like—and how well association leaders understand and appeal to Millennials.

The tendency of Millennials to "associate" does not at all mean that existing associations have an easy path ahead. Many of the new Millennial associational genres involve new technologies, new interests, new causes, new corners of the culture. Older people (especially those still pursuing grand causes) may be frustrated with how these kids pay scant attention to those old causes and instead cut through to something new. Goodbye, Kiwanis. Hello, Buddy Lists. The smart association will be one that finds a way to tap into the distinctly "modern," 21st century aspect of this new generational mindset. You may need to step aside a little and let them organize a few things their own way.

— **William Strauss**
Co-author, *Millennials Rising*
Guest Expert, ASAE Foundation Futures Scan Community of Practice

Opportunities for Synergy

Tensions exist wherever there are differences. Generational differences are no exception. But where there's tension, energy abounds. And where there's energy, there's opportunity for synergy.

Each generation has, in some way, enabled the development of subsequent generations. Each generation has distinctive contributions to make. And each generation can interact with other generations to accomplish something it couldn't do on its own. Here are examples of generational synergy, as seen from the perspective of the three main generations currently active in the association world.

LIFELINE EXERCISE: SHARING GENERATIONAL EXPERIENCES

Use this 45- to 60-minute exercise with small (6–8 person), mixed-generation groups. Begin by giving each person a sheet of paper with a time line on it running from his or her birth to the present day.

/_____/_____/_____/_____/_____/_____/

Birth   Today

Ask participants to take five minutes to reflect on the life experiences that have had the greatest influence on their outlooks and to write those experiences on their time line. Have participants share their time lines; encourage them to ask questions and discuss each other's experiences. As a group, spend 10 minutes discussing the extent to which many of these experiences were generational in character as opposed to personal and unique.

Silents

Over the next 10 years, many Silents will be nearing the end of long careers with their associations. With lengthening "health spans" as well as life spans, some could remain involved in association life even longer. Encourage Silents to remain active in flexible capacities because your association will probably need their distinctive competencies: communicating, negotiating, mentoring, resolving disputes, and facilitating the interactions of other generations.

One role Silents can potentially play is mediating between Boomers and X-ers. Silents can speak to Boomers as peers, or elders, but they don't elicit the kind of stigmatized response from X-ers that Boomers often do. They know Boomers well because they have worked with them and mediated between Boomers and the GI generation for decades. They can empathize with X-ers because of their own life experience. Having grown up overshadowed by both the GI Generation and the Boomers, Silents are very familiar with the struggle of finding identity while sandwiched between two dominant generations.

Just as children sometimes find their grandparents more sympathetic than their parents, X-ers find that Silents can sometimes see who they are more clearly than Boomers. Silents are less likely to view X-ers as slackers and more likely to appreciate that generation's agility and energy. Silents can be ambassadors for X-ers, helping communicate their views to Boomers. They can also be mentors, helping X-ers get ahead in organizations dominated by Boomers. As nonwork aspects of life become more important for aging Silents, they may appreciate more fully—and endorse—the desire of many X-ers to lead balanced lives.

Boomers

Always an idealistic but conflicted group, Baby Boomers have a common denominator in creating a worthwhile legacy. In *Generations, The Fourth Turning*, and other books, William Strauss and Neil Howe argue that throughout American history the generations that were most idealistic and challenged the established order in their youth actually made their greatest contributions through principled and inspirational "elder stewardship." They passed on the best, most time-tested aspects of their youthful idealism to younger generations.

The greatest opportunity Boomers in the association community have for elder stewardship is the recruitment and mentoring of Millennials. It is up to Boomers to create an association environment that the dynamic Millennial Generation wants to join. For associations with younger

---

REVERSE MENTORING

In addition to mentoring younger people in your organization, consider "reverse mentoring"—developing relationships where the primary intent is to look at your association from the perspective of a Generation X staff member. Your first instinct may be to set up a 7 a.m. "power breakfast" at an upscale restaurant. Your Gen X mentor, however, would probably choose a different place. Let your mentor bring you into his or her world.

members, this challenge has begun; for most others, it approaches within a decade. This will require a willingness to step aside enough to let Millennials organize around their own interests and priorities.

In *Millennials Rising*, William Strauss and Neil Howe warn that the enormous potential of the Millennial Generation could go awry if future developments thwart its aspirations or mobilize it around a risky, even destructive, national agenda. The Baby Boom Generation has a critical leadership role to play: enlisting the ambition and aspiration of Millennials in the pursuit of constructive purposes and larger challenges than they have yet faced.

HOW BOOMERS CAN CULTIVATE GEN X RELATIONSHIPS

- Give them flexibility to accommodate different aspects of their lives.
  - Hold meetings and conferences at activity-oriented sites.
  - Incorporate mechanisms like flextime.
  - Show them that you, too, have other priorities in your life; minimize the notion that "you don't understand."
- Affirm how they are making a difference by using concrete examples and giving explicit feedback.
  - Give regular performance reviews with praise for jobs well-done and specific suggestions for improvement.
  - When they've exceeded the call of duty, reward X-ers with tangible compensation, ranging from gift certificates to opportunities for professional development.
- Create learning opportunities to help them increase their skills.
  - Hold team meetings where everyone has the opportunity to give direct feedback on "lessons learned" from different projects and to contribute new ideas, regardless of position or years of service.
  - When critiquing work, use a "consultative" approach; foster growth according to their own style, rather than imposing/reworking their work according to your style.
  - Make information available; know your stuff so that you can provide correct facts and figures.
- Incorporate their "realistic" approach into your organization's mission statement. Use survivalist language (as opposed to empowerment lingo), emphasizing traits of efficiency, achievement of objectives, and bottom-line results.

Boomers will dominate the political agenda for a generation. Will Boomers create a Shangri-la in their maturity or "Jurassic Park"? It depends on whether they vote increasingly and disproportionately to benefit themselves or are able to recapture their idealism and act for the benefit of younger generations and the society as a whole.

— **Ken Dychtwald**
  Author, *Age Power*
  Guest Expert, ASAE Foundation Futures Scan Community of Practice

As Boomers consider how to inspire and support the accomplishments of another generation, instead of focusing on themselves, they are more likely to appreciate X-ers. If a Boomer executive *really* cares about leaving a legacy, the most helpful person may well be right before her eyes: that rumpled, Starbucks-drinking X-er. In an increasingly accountability-driven environment, Boomers have a huge asset in the honest feedback of their X-er cohorts, who are not intimidated by authority. And, more important for Boomers, X-ers are likely to give them realistic, tough-minded advice about how to build a legacy.

Boomers need to abandon the traditional notion that years at a job or years of volunteer service equate to positions of authority. If Boomers hang on to positions of authority by virtue of seniority alone, they will block the advancement of younger generations and the potential for generational synergy. In that situation, Millennials might simply choose to bypass existing associations and create their own.

The need for generational diversity is especially great in association governance. Boomers will gain enormous respect from younger generations if they insist on competence and accomplishment as the criteria for advancement.

Boomers hold the key to creating worthwhile legacies and shaping the future of associations. They must appreciate the importance of creating an environment in which X-ers and Millennials are enthusiastic about working together with them to make their legacies concrete, their ideals a reality.

X-ers

As X-ers enter their midlife years, some of their best characteristics are becoming more evident. They are adaptable and feedback-oriented and have a pragmatic survival mentality. They accept—and value—diversity. In conversation, they often cut quickly to the core of an issue. They don't want to waste time or do things that don't make sense. They need to know that whatever they are doing has meaning and purpose.

The challenging nature of X-ers to always ask "why" can be extremely valuable if applied correctly to planning and innovation. While Boomers speak with idealism, X-ers are more inclined to turn to the challenge at hand and provide hands-on, get-it-done leadership. In associations, they are most likely to be the risk-takers who will work for changes they think are important, unhindered by their current environment.

As Boomers become more appreciative of the qualities and potential contributions of X-ers, the younger generation will need to point the

---

GENERATIONAL SYNERGY IN ACTION

The Boston-based organization Youth on Board helps organizations introduce young people to positions of power and responsibility. Here are some highlights of a Youth on Board publication titled *14 Points: Successfully Involving Youth in Decision Making.*

- Know why you want to involve younger people in governance structure. There are many good reasons, but each board must reflect its own organizational goals and interests.

- Identify potential barriers from individuals, the organizational culture, and the association's own bylaws.

- Conduct intergenerational training to sharpen skills of relationship building, listening, and communicating.

- Adopt strategies that support and develop younger leaders by helping them deal with outside forces and enabling them to network with each other.

MAKING ROOM FOR X-ER LEADERSHIP

"Your youth is your strength. In the next period of your life you'll be confronted with more rules, processes, mores, and traditions than you ever thought possible…. When you're trying to change something for the better, it's often easier to ask for forgiveness than permission. Act now, apologize later. A little well-planned irreverence will take you a long way."
—Adam Werbach, former Sierra Club President

In May 1996, the nation's oldest environmental organization recognized the importance of new perspectives and generational characteristics. Specifically, the 650,000-member Sierra Club realized that, for the environmental movement to grow, it was time to appeal and listen to younger voices. The first step in this direction was for some of the Boomer leadership to move aside and to elect Adam Werbach, a 23-year-old, as president.

The Sierra Club took a risk, but its approach was fruitful. Fully aware of his generation, Werbach appealed to them through hard-hitting messages and local action, all with an accent on multiculturalism. Although Werbach's Gen X approach drew scattered criticism, under his leadership the Sierra Club received more press attention. That, in turn, led to increased membership and donations. In addition, the average age of a member decreased by a decade. Werbach's term was not all about flash and youthful energy. Under his leadership, the Sierra Club forged the campaign to pass the strongest clean air standards in America's history.

Reflecting the independence and impatience of his generation, Werbach stepped down from his post, stating that he was frustrated with the Sierra Club—"not with the good work we were doing but at the pace of change."

hypocritical finger back at themselves and ask, "Where did my ideas to do my own thing come from? Who created this environment where I can be an individual?" If X-ers are to walk *their* talk, they can begin by recognizing the substantive outcomes of the Boomer movements that give them the freedom to operate within expansive boundaries. Acknowledging their predecessors' contribution will release tensions that X-ers have often created in their relationship with Boomers.

Provocative Questions
For Association Executives and Leaders

The "generational constellation" in associations today includes three main groups: the Silent Generation, the Baby Boom Generation, and Generation X. The once-dominant GI Generation has almost left the scene, but the Millennial Generation (born after 1981) will soon enter the workplace in full force. A better understanding of the life experiences and outlooks of each of these generations is necessary for bringing them into creative interaction. Each generation has distinctive contributions to make and roles it can play to support other generations.

1. People in each generation need to know something of the life experiences, outlooks, and motivations of each of the other generations around them. In what ways can your association facilitate greater understanding? Where do you have tensions now?

2. Encouraging individuals from different generations to contribute their special strengths will enable your association to attract and hold four generations in synergy. Are you taking full advantage of the distinctive attributes individuals can bring to your volunteer committees, task forces, and staff teams?

3. Millennials promise to become the greatest institution builders since the GI Generation. They could rejuvenate associations. Will Millennials find your association attractive and inclusive to their generation? What can you do to make your association more attractive to Millennials?

4. With longer, healthier life spans, Silents could remain involved in association life longer. In what flexible capacities could you use their skills in communicating, negotiating, mentoring, resolving disputes, and facilitating?

5. The greatest opportunity Boomers in the association community have for elder stewardship is the recruitment and mentoring of Millennials. How might Boomers be the champions of the changes Millennials will seek in your association? Are they ready to step aside for Gen X-ers to become leaders?

6. Gen X-ers are most likely to be the risk takers who will work for changes they think are important. How might they be used in resolving your association's most intractable challenges?

7. Boomers and Gen X-ers often have negative stereotypes of each other. What can you do in your day-to-day activity to counteract these stereotypes?

Provocative Questions
For Business Partners

The pattern of generations in associations today includes three main groups: the Silent Generation, the Baby Boom Generation, and Generation X. A better understanding of the life experiences and outlooks of each of these generations is necessary for bringing them into creative interaction. Business partners that learn to foster intergenerational synergy will gain enormous advantages.

1. Become familiar with the distinct needs of each generation in your market. Do your products and services bridge their interests? Would some be better received if they were customized for different generations? Are you content to serve some generations and not others?

2. Recognize areas of synergy that you can help facilitate through your products and services.

3. Look to consciously create synergy. Your clients are not necessarily looking for mirror images of themselves, they may be looking for a fresh generational perspective. Can you market experience and stability to younger customers and clients? Can you offer a youthful edginess to an established client?

4. Remember, society overall is aging. Do your products and services accommodate this trend (for example, bigger print, accessibility, diet, opportunities for engaging experiences)?

Recommended Resources

Age Power: How the 21st Century Will Be Ruled by the New Old, by Ken Dychtwald (JP Tarcher, 1999). Describes the social, political, and economic implications of the aging of the Baby Boomers.

The Fourth Turning, by Neil Howe and William Strauss (Broadway, 1998). An in-depth presentation of the four generational archetypes and how their interaction generates cyclical historical patterns.

Generation 2K, by Wendy Murray Zoba (Intervarsity, 1999). A balanced exploration of the values and the moral ambivalence of the Millennial Generation.

Generation X: The Young Adult Market, by Susan Mitchell (New Strategist, 1997). Detailed demographic analysis of Generation X spending patterns.

Generations at Work, by Ron Zemke, Claire Raines, and Bob Filipczak (Amacom, 1999). Instructions on helping integrate four generations into an organization.

Growing Up Digital: The Rise of the Net Generation, by Don Tapscott (McGraw-Hill, 1998). Labels the Millennials as the "Net Generation" and focuses on their rapid adoption and integration of computer and communications technology.

Millennials Rising: The Next Great Generation, by Neil Howe and William Strauss (Vintage, 2000). A hopeful description of the Millennial Generation and its potential role as the next "great" generation.

Rocking the Ages: The Yankelovich Report on Generational Marketing, by Walker Smith and Ann Clurman (HarperBusiness, 1997). A review and synthesis of 30 years of generational data gathered by the Yankelovich polling organization, identifying key similarities and differences among Silents, Boomers, and Gen X-ers.

The X-ers & the Boomers: From Adversaries to Allies, by Claire Raines (Crisp, 2000). Aims at resolving generational conflicts in the workplace, leading the reader through a communication process that can bridge the generation gap.

CHAPTER 5
Learning Culture

Learning Culture: A learner-centered education environment facilitating collaborative learning processes that can be pursued at any time, from any location.

The ability to learn is emerging as the most important skill individuals and institutions need to thrive amid rapid change and to cope with the opportunities and challenges of the 21st century. Older models of education are becoming less relevant in an economy that values skills and ability more than formal credentials.

A constant evolution of skills is needed to adapt to the rapid changes in technology and the economy. New understandings are emerging of the social and psychological conditions that foster effective learning. At the same time, vast quantities of educational resources are available online. This signals the development of a learning culture that extends far beyond classrooms and into everyday life. From stopping global warming to fostering equitable and sustainable development, societal challenges can be met only by collectively "learning our way" into the future.

In the learning culture taking shape, the educational focus for associations is shifting away from *teaching* and is instead turning toward *learning*. As a result, the traditional models of continuing education will gradually give way to continuous learning. The information landscape is becoming increasingly crowded, with schools, for-profit instructional programs, and industries providing an expanding range of educational offerings. Associations can maintain their value to members by moving beyond their role of teacher to become a facilitator of learning. Associations can play an important role as a nexus of communication, acting as the central hub in a network of learners.

IMPLICATIONS FOR ASSOCIATIONS	ACTION STEPS
• Learning is moving away from fact-based instruction toward models of active learning in which knowledge and meaning are collaboratively and actively constructed. • Taking risks, running experiments, making mistakes, catching them quickly, and learning all you can from them is the best strategy for rapid learning and innovation. • Distributed learning puts the learner at the center of the learning process. • The emerging learning culture has more to do with the support and promotion of continuous learning than continuing education.	• Adopt assessment methods to keep credentialing programs relevant to active learning. • Create a safe environment where members feel secure enough to admit uncertainty and share failures. • Use communication technologies to customize the learner's experience. • Model a learning culture in working with staff and volunteer leaders.

Schools are at a competitive disadvantage because of the inertia implied in maintaining a formal curriculum, the need to attract and keep expert faculties, and the large investment in physical plant, which can interfere with offering flexible, responsive extended learning support services. Associations do not face these same constraints and are well-positioned to play a central role in supporting the learning of their members. However, the need for learning isn't limited to the membership—association leaders will need to embrace continuous learning to stay one step ahead in a rapidly changing world.

If associations do not provide the type of learning experiences members want, someone else will.

— Don I. Tharpe, Ed.D.
Executive Director, Association of School Business Officials, International

Traditionally, associations' educational activities have more to do with information transfer than with real *learning*. Learning is a far more complex, challenging, and complicated process than some associations are equipped to handle. What learning will matter most in the future that association members are preparing to shape? What will be required to shift from delivering education programs to creating a learning culture?

The emerging learning culture has four key characteristics: meaningful information, active learning, learning amid uncertainty, and distributed learning.

Meaningful Information

With the multiplication of alternative media channels, widespread use of the personal computer, and the explosive growth of the Internet, the quantity of data has become immense. We are increasingly faced with *infoglut*—a deluge of information that can obscure valuable, meaningful knowledge. What's important gets lost in the sheer volume of information available.

The relationship among data, information, and knowledge can be viewed hierarchically, with filters at each level. The resulting pyramid—with data, information, and knowledge stacked on top of one another—is capped by wisdom and application.

At the base of the pyramid are data—undigested observations and raw facts presented without a directly relevant context. Next comes information, where someone else has organized raw data into a more meaningful and understandable form. Then comes knowledge, in which organized information is integrated into the specific and unique knowledge and interests of an individual. Finally comes wisdom and application—making connections between separate areas of knowledge to create a superstructure of understanding and putting the new knowledge to good use.

Filtering information and giving it a context make it more meaningful. For instance, Web portals such as Excite, Alta Vista, and Yahoo have attracted massive audiences because they categorize and index the wealth of information available online. With the billions of Web pages available, any given bit of information is almost irrelevant unless the raw data are reconfigured into a meaningful context.

The search engine Google even measures how *meaningful* a Web site is to the overall Internet community. Google calculates the number of other Web sites that link to an association's site and uses that statistic for ranking the relevance of keyword searches.

Traditionally, associations have provided a valuable function to their members by accumulating and disseminating information. Association members, however, now face a relentless barrage of information—and association publications run the risk of adding to their members' sense of being overwhelmed. Simply providing *more* information to members or customers only contributes to infoglut. But information that has been filtered for relevance, assessed for accuracy, and customized to the needs and preferences of members will remain meaningful.

Although the ability to individually tailor all member materials remains an elusive ideal, associations can increase the degree of customization and thus increase meaning. This requires developing a better understanding of the unique information and knowledge needs among members. More extensive use of member surveys or market segmentation data can help identify member constituencies with unique information needs. Once identified, these groups can be given the most relevant, targeted information.

Active Learning

Learning facts—and being able to repeat them on tests—remains the dominant approach to education. Although some factual learning is necessary, several forces are moving education away from an exclusive focus on fact-based education.

The relevance of fact-based education diminishes when new breakthroughs continuously reshape the landscape of knowledge. Accelerating technical innovation creates a situation where entire scientific fields are in a state of perpetual flux. In nonscientific fields, this trend manifests itself in the sheer volume of intellectual activity. Although it's possible to keep fully abreast of developments in a small niche, tracking ongoing developments in an entire field is impossible.

INFORMATION THAT COUNTS

Here are three ways associations can ensure the information they provide their members is meaningful.

Legitimize—Is the information relevant and accurate?
Establish peer-review processes, seals of approval, or certification programs for content providers in your industry or profession. Help your members sort the wheat from the chaff.

Customize—How can I get only the information I want, in the way I want it?
Ask your members about their preferences. What kinds of information are they most interested in? What delivery methods do they prefer? How often do they want to receive it? Do different segments of your membership have different preferences? Be prepared to respond to their answers.

Synthesize—What's really important and what does all this information mean?
Don't overwhelm members with a high volume of e-mails, meeting announcements, and disconnected pieces of information in the belief that this will demonstrate your value. Rather, put your effort into communicating truly important information well. Whenever possible, make connections between ideas and events and help your members see a big picture of what's happening in their field.

ELEMENTS OF A LEARNING CULTURE

Since the publication of Peter Senge's *The Fifth Discipline* in 1990, the concept of the learning organization has begun to take root. A growing body of evidence from organizational research identifies a core set of practices adopted by organizations that are able to be adaptive and innovative over extended periods of time. These characteristics include:

- A concern for people, including an equal concern for all stakeholders.

- A belief that people are willing to learn and can value learning for its own sake.

- A shared belief that the world is malleable and that it's possible to shape our own fate.

- Enough diversity in groups and organizational subcultures to allow the formulation of meaningfully alternative points of view.

- A shared commitment to transparent communication, ensuring that all the relevant information can be honestly disclosed and discussed.

- A shared commitment to systems thinking that emphasizes multiple causes and feedback loops.

- A shared belief that teams and groups can produce better results than individual effort.

At its core, learning is a process of making meaning around our experiences. We experience something and we seek to understand what it means to us relative to our previous experiences. Looking at it through this lens, we can see learning as a highly personal process of developing deeper relationships with ourselves, with ideas and concepts, with other people, and so on. Moreover, we can see learning as a process of changing our thinking so that we can design more effective action, instead of as a process of "changing behavior," which is the dominant perspective held by association educators.

— Jeff De Cagna
Managing Director, Strategic Learning and Development, Special Libraries Association

Both the pace of change and changing views of the nature of knowledge call for more emphasis on the *process of learning* itself. From this perspective, learning is a form of active mental work that involves the construction of new ideas and associations, not the passive reception of data. Learners are not empty, passive vessels into which knowledge can be poured; they actively construct their understanding of the world, validating and cross-checking their images of reality through social interaction with peers. Association members have, in many ways, done this for years. They typically turn to their peers to gain insight into how to address similar situations and then piece together those various perspectives to guide their own decision making.

These "constructivist" theories of active learning have been integrated into the curriculum of some primary and secondary schools. High schools, for instance, have begun to adopt study circles similar to those used in law schools. In some cases, final essay questions are given out weeks in advance, and students are encouraged to collaborate in formulating their answers. These study groups allow the "answers" to be discovered through a collective process of exploration and give students first-hand exposure to the learning strategies and mental models of their peers.

Under the old paradigm of fact-based learning, this sort of cooperation would be regarded as cheating. In a learning culture, it becomes a powerful technique for promoting group learning.

An active approach to learning finds common ground between divergent ideas, rather than focusing on exchanging differential facts to convince the "wrong" party of the "facts" that are known to be "right." The latter approach often leads to a futile debate that never addresses the underlying premises. Instead, embracing the idea that knowledge is a mental construction makes it possible to gain additional perspective on the issues.

One virtue of active learning exercises is that they can push learners to shift mental models much more rapidly than conventional instructional methods. For years, Edward Deming, the world-renowned quality expert, used an exercise to illustrate a point about system dynamics. He filled a box with 3,200 white balls and 800 red balls. Six volunteers from the audience were each given a flat paddle with 50 small holes and told to use the paddles to fill customers' orders for only white balls. Accountability standards were set for the six volunteers, incentives were created to reward the top producers, and bottom producers faced the threat of being fired.

As the simulation progressed, the established system created anxiety. The best performers became concerned that they could not keep up their performance. Participants who fell behind, through no fault of their own, experienced frustration and anger. Inevitably, a few red balls would show up in the final "product" despite the workers' best intentions.

A RAPID RESPONSE

One guest participant in the ASAE Foundation Online Community of Practice was Scott Beatty, a knowledge manager at Royal Dutch/Shell who shared some of his experiences in generating active learning:

"We have a program called Focused Results Delivery (FRD); this 90-day program blends the achievement of hard business results with an in-depth investigation of leadership, change management, culture, and the structures that drive behavior. Teams are given a business problem and given 90 days to deliver a quantum improvement in that portion of the business. We guarantee 25 times cost so we deal only with high-value business problems.

"We had one group that had nine teams in the refining end of the U.S. business. The teams had to learn how to achieve faster, better, cheaper ways of doing business and then implement them across the organization. Rather than doing things nine different ways in nine different refineries, we have common approaches to the same issue. We conduct four workshops over the 90 days where content learning is blended with leadership learning. In the nine-team FRD we did in the U.S., we were able to identify and deliver $170 million dollars in results improvement."

These "rapid response" learning teams obtain their results and improve learning capacities though direct collaboration. They don't solve problems for co-workers—they solve problems *with* them. How could rapid response learning teams work in an association context? Could national organizations send teams to chapters or member companies? What sort of problems would benefit from a learning team? How could their deployment become a genuine learning experience, not just a quick fix?

By the end of the exercise, the participants had experienced first-hand the lesson that badly designed processes can undermine the work of even skilled and motivated workers. Deming used this exercise to illustrate a complex point: Raising standards and increasing incentives and penalties—without fundamentally changing the system—does not dramatically increase quality and robs participants of a sense of responsibility and pride in their work. The exercise conveyed an essential insight with dramatic clarity.

BEHAVIOR TO ENCOURAGE LEARNING

Learners may fear the wide-ranging mental explorations that are integral to developing new and innovative ideas. The fear of the unknown, or anxiety about finding incorrect answers, often limits learners to the realm of simple certainties. Associations can apply the following principles to create an environment that minimizes the anxiety of uncertainty and nurtures innovation:

- Provide a supportive and psychologically affirming environment.

- Rather than threaten with disaster, use a positive vision of a better future to inspire learning efforts.

- Create a "practice field" where learners are encouraged to make mistakes and learn from them.

- Provide some basic direction and guidance to help get learners moving in the right direction.

- Support collaborative learning—the camaraderie of a group can help alleviate the fears of exploring the unknown.

- Provide good coaching and constructive feedback.

- Reward the smallest positive steps forward instead of punishing mistakes.

- Don't avoid errors. Embrace them, because they enable us to learn.

- Avoid assigning blame when mistakes occur. Instead, focus on lessons learned that can be applied in the future.

Sensitivity to mental models doesn't necessarily mean dismissing issues with a nonchalant, "It's all relative." Finding and identifying the underlying premises behind ideas becomes the primary route for creating shared understanding. Understanding the mental models of others helps facilitate effective collaboration between individuals or groups that disagree. Merely determining the right questions to address can often be more productive than answering the wrong question. Associations can facilitate a deeper and more significant form of collaboration to explore differences in underlying assumptions, which are often unconsciously held. They can help their members ask the right questions.

The rise of active learning poses a major challenge for association training, credentialing, and licensing activities. Training and testing are relatively straightforward, with fact-based instructional methods, but become increasingly problematic as learning grows more active and collaborative. Standardized tests and exams are designed to test the retention of facts, not the deeper understanding derived from collaborative learning processes.

Outcome-based mechanisms are becoming popular in schools as a means of assessing learning. More elaborate active learning activities use periodic assessments of an integrated portfolio of work or peer-review panels to gauge progress. Associations will have to adopt similar assessment methods—or entirely new methods—to keep credentialing programs relevant in a time of accelerating change.

Learning Amid Uncertainty

Traditional learning approaches typically elevate the fear of failing, largely because institutions can easily manipulate incentives and disincentives. In schools, the threat of poor grades is used to motivate learning; in the workplace, the possibility of being passed over for promotion can motivate employees to overcome their reluctance to change.

In a learning culture, amplifying fears of failure can impede innovative and creative thinking. The incentive structures must change by reducing the anxiety associated with the unknown. This approach motivates learners to feel more comfortable about trying something new.

If learners test new approaches to knowledge, some of their experiments inevitably will turn out to be mistakes. In traditional approaches to learning, mistakes are judged as "failures"—something to be avoided at all costs. A learning culture, however, treats errors as a necessary part of the learning process. A learning culture has no failure—only feedback. Taking risks, running experiments, making mistakes, catching them quickly, and learning all you can from them is the best strategy for rapid learning and innovation.

Silicon Valley during the 1990s exemplified this attitude toward innovation and uncertainty. Workers jumped from one employer to another, often working at one place for no longer than six months. The companies ranged from tenuous start-ups, to entrepreneurial independent businesses, to groups of friends working out of their bedrooms. These "disposable companies" often left a trail of failed business experiments on the resumes of workers. But because of a widespread willingness to take risks and learn from mistakes, Silicon Valley was able to experiment with new business ideas and consequently increase the pace of innovation.

The feedback that comes from wrong approaches and incorrect answers is necessary for innovative and creative thinking that can successfully navigate change. After all, once an organization's leaders believe they have discovered "the right answer," the natural inclination is to keep applying that solution indefinitely. Business literature is filled with stories of organizations that found a solution to their business concerns and kept using that solution as the marketplace evolved. They became victims of their own success, because they projected their successful solutions into the foreseeable future rather than continuously learning and adapting.

A learning culture emphasizes learning from any and all sources, including learning from mistakes rather than avoiding them. The mistakes, errors, shortcomings, and even failures that interrupt established patterns of success help clear the way for new possibilities. A mistake is a golden opportunity for reassessment, because it allows you to use the feedback and lessons learned in formulating a new solution.

If association board and staff members focus exclusively on avoiding mistakes, they will miss important opportunities and never approach the leading edge of innovation and adaptation. The key to accelerating association innovation is establishing a shared understanding that mistakes are acceptable—as long as they are identified and corrected quickly and their learning is applied to future efforts.

Associations also can deliberately create an environment where their members feel secure enough to *admit uncertainty*. It is always easy to share successes; the association fostering real learning makes it comfortable to discuss and learn from mistakes, too. This frank and open exchange enables members to drop their guard and ask the important questions for which there are no easy answers.

Distributed Learning

Distributed learning puts the student at the center of the learning process. Unlike schools, which must overcome the institutional inertia of preserving a physical campus and an approved curriculum, associations have the opportunity to offer educational services in a distributed fashion. Because many association "students" must fit continuing education on top of a full-time job, they form a natural market for distributed learning.

Distributed learning takes advantage of the growing convergence of digital media: Text, audio, film, video—even historical documents—can be digitized and distributed online. Some associations and educational institutions are moving beyond supplementing traditional classes with Internet content to putting the entire educational experience online. By 2010, for example, the Massachusetts Institute of Technology plans to make the content of all courses publicly available for free on the Web.

Another pioneer is Cardean University, a virtual business college that combines offerings from the business schools of Carnegie-Mellon, Columbia, Stanford, the University of Chicago, and the London School of Economics. Cardean offers complete business courses for full-time workers who wish to learn in the evening, on the weekends, or whenever. Eventually it plans to offer a full program that will allow students to study for an MBA without ever setting foot in the classroom.

When such experiments in online learning use the traditional model of "sage on a stage" instruction, they do little more than overcome physical distance in learning. Like educational television and satellite conferencing before the Internet, they are providing education in a controlled setting, at a predetermined time, using standardized instructional materials. What's necessary is to re-purpose existing curriculum for a distributed learning model. The real challenge is accepting the fundamental premise: rely less on information transfer and focus more on learner-constructed meaning.

The degree to which distributed learning will overshadow traditional education delivery relies on the communications bandwidth. The greater the degree of bandwidth available, the greater the richness and realism of the virtual learning environments. Today's technology already supports basic distributed learning activities. E-mail lists and Web-based discussion systems, for example, allow participants to share insights with a community of like-minded learners. Web-based educational resources can become more than just established links to sources of information. They are increasingly able to become forums for distributed learning.

DISTRIBUTED LEARNING IN ACTION

Distributed learning activities don't have to take place within an elaborate online curriculum or use sophisticated computer conferencing tools. All that's necessary is a community of learners able to interact with one another independent of geography or a specific schedule. The listserves sponsored by the American Society of Association Executives (ASAE) are one example of a low-tech implementation of learner-led distributed learning.

Members may join any of ASAE's Internet-based discussion groups that are nominally hosted by the various special interest groups (SIGs). These unstructured communication forums enable any interested member to post questions, requests, or referrals. Other participants respond by posting responses on the listserve (which can be read by any other participant) or by direct e-mail to the person making the request.

Education consultant Chip Levy finds this distributed learning activity to be an important association benefit: "I'm always interested in watching the flow of question-response-response-response. Somebody will post a question, and within a matter of hours there will invariably be several responses. Some address the initial posting, some elaborate on others' responses—but all are from other practitioners who have directly applicable experience. Some responses may be terse, while others are quite thoughtful; some basic, some higher-level. Some responses are better than others, to be sure, but they're all from colleagues. And they can come from anywhere—it's not uncommon to have responses from various parts of the country and, increasingly, from other parts of the world. Access to that venue alone is worth the cost of my annual dues."

One example of a new direction is Webquests, a learning tool created at San Diego State University. Webquests are inquiry-driven activities that create a framework for an individual or groups to construct meaningful knowledge out of Internet information resources. A Webquest provides background information and presents tasks for learners to perform: creating a report, editing an imaginary newspaper, or preparing slides for a presentation.

What if associations were able to instantly distill and redistribute the collective experience and developing knowledge of its membership in real time? What if associations were able to focus learning to simultaneously develop and disperse new knowledge? The ASAE Foundation online discussions showed this to be possible. Every day, the participants brought something new to the table and walked away with even more.

— **Robert A. Teplansky**
Principal, New Community Associates

Often these tasks are wrapped up in an attention-grabbing theme that involves hypothetical scenarios, characters, or roles. An integrated resources section contains a targeted list of links to Internet resources that contain information directly relevant to the task. A concluding section provides overall guidance, offering tips, insightful questions, and possible approaches that will keep the learners on course. In Webquests, the actual process of *learning* occurs within and between individual learners as they interpret, shape, and present the information to complete the task.

Association staffers have long observed how much learning happens in the hallways at conferences and seminars. Astute associations will facilitate greater interaction and connection to the wisdom in the group. Powerful group learning occurs when people can move beyond technical material and are able to push out against their usual "comfort zones" and talk about lifetime aspirations, fears of criticism and failure, and personal struggles to close the gap between their "business selves" and their "true selves." Opportunities for active learning will increasingly displace today's lecture sessions at education conferences. In the future, associations will measure the success of their education programs by how much learning *the group* generated.

With a premium placed on group learning, associations must pay close attention to having office and meeting space that favors human interaction. What will be the design of the hallways of the future convention center if they are passageways to learning and interaction? If collaboration matters most, the premium space in offices will go to common areas rather than corner offices.

Web sites, online learning, and group learning experiences are the forerunners of distributed learning techniques. The emerging learning culture has more to do with the support and promotion of continuous learning rather than continuing education.

The key to understanding mediated communication is that it complements face-to-face interaction rather than substituting for it. Possibilities for face-to-face interactions among members of associations are scant in comparison to their professional lives; it makes sense to look for powerful ways to supplement direct human contact.

— Chris Dede
Endowed Chair in Educational Technology, Harvard University
Guest Expert, ASAE Foundation Futures Scan Community Practice

Provocative Questions
For Association Executives and Leaders

The educational focus for associations is shifting away from transfer of information and teaching toward continuous learning. Associations will become facilitators of learning, acting as the central hub in a network of learners. Their education programs will employ active learning and use distributed learning to engage participants wherever they are located.

1. Associations can filter information for relevance, assess it for accuracy, and customize it to members' needs and preferences. How can you make your association's information more accessible for the individual learner's use?

2. Both the pace of change and changing views of the nature of knowledge will lead toward styles of learning that emphasize the *process of learning* itself. What is your association doing to help your members become better learners?

3. Associations can facilitate a deeper and more significant form of collaboration to explore differences in underlying assumptions, which are often unconsciously held. How are you intentionally helping members explore their mental models and get to the right questions?

4. Active learning approaches pose a major challenge for association training, credentialing, and licensing activities. What methods of assessment might you use to evaluate knowledge and performance in a world where facts are less relevant than new learning?

5. Taking risks, running experiments, making mistakes, catching them quickly, and learning all you can from them is the best strategy for rapid learning and innovation. How might your association facilitate rapid learning and innovation within your membership?

6. Instead of motivating learning by increasing the fear of failing, we need to motivate learners to feel more comfortable about trying new things. How might your association create a safe environment for members to take risks, share failures, and try new things?

7. Distributed learning builds on the mental models of a diverse and heterogeneous group to create a more robust learning experience. How can new technologies be used to facilitate learner-constructed meaning?

8. In the future, associations will measure the success of their education programs by how much learning the *group* generated. Can your association claim its future role as a facilitator of a network of learners shaping knowledge for your field? What measures of success will ensure that your members are the leaders in learning?

Provocative Questions
For Business Partners

The ability to *learn* is emerging as the most important skill that individuals and institutions need to thrive amid rapid change and cope with the opportunities and challenges of the 21st century. Associations are positioned to be both a more important learning resource for their members and a driving force in the creation of a learning culture.

1. The facilities that associations use must be designed around collaborative learning. How can you create environments for learning that help sell your product or service?

2. Creating a distributed learning infrastructure will be a significant market for association business partners. What aspects of this potential business can you secure?

3. Business partners that currently have no educational component to their goods and services will have new opportunities to bundle a learning component into their offerings. How might you rethink your products and services in terms of a learning culture?

4. Fact-based instructional programs or services need to be reformulated to meet the need for collaborative learning among association members. What expertise can you lend to this major undertaking?

5. Business partners have to do their part to create safe learning environments that will help association learners explore uncertainty, innovation, and experimentation. How comfortable are you with sharing failures and taking risks in a competitive marketplace?

6. As a business partner you may have a different mental models than the majority of the association's members. How might you constructively share these perspectives to improve the active learning of the entire membership?

Recommended Resources

The Fifth Discipline: The Art and Practice of the Learning Organization, by Peter Senge (Doubleday, 1994). A business classic that highlights the importance of learning for the contemporary organization.

Learning in Action: A Guide to Putting the Learning Organization to Work, by David A. Garvin (Harvard Business School Press, 2000). Analyzes the activities of existing learning organizations and outlines the steps necessary to build one.

Learning Organizations, edited by Sarita Chawla and John Renesch (Productivity Press, 1995). A collection of essays by thinkers on the leading edge of organizational learning.

Serious Play: How the World's Best Companies Simulate to Innovate, by Michael Schrage (Harvard Business School Press, 2000). Describes how innovative companies are using simulations and experiential learning to facilitate group learning.

The Social Life of Information, by John Seely Brown and Paul Duguid (Harvard Business School Press, 2000). Emphasizes the human aspects of knowledge creation that are often overlooked in information technology discussions.

The Webquest Page. Background information and instructional materials on using Webquests as an educational tool (http://edweb.sdsu.edu/webquest/webquest.html).

CHAPTER 6
Transparency

Transparency: Operating in an open and accountable manner; providing the public with information it can use to evaluate an organization's performance.

*T*ransparency involves operating in an open, accountable manner and providing the public with information it can use to evaluate your performance. Association members, and associations themselves, will be forced to develop deliberate "transparency strategies" because pressures for openness and accountability are growing rapidly, driven by the spread of democracy, economic globalization, the digital revolution, and the rise of Internet-enhanced social activism.

In developing positions on this issue, associations need to balance the advantages of greater openness with their members' legitimate concerns about the appropriate limits and the dangers of revealing too much.

Transparency's Inevitability

The trend toward greater transparency will continue because powerful forces are driving it. These forces are unlikely to diminish over the generation ahead.

The Spread of Democracy. At the beginning of the 20th century, monarchies and empires still dominated the world; about 12 percent of the world's population participated in democratic processes. At the beginning of the 21st century, nearly 60 percent of the world's population lives in some form of electoral democracy.

IMPLICATIONS FOR ASSOCIATIONS	ACTION STEPS
• New values of openness and accountability are spreading around the globe and touching every organization.	• Discuss transparency-related issues with key stakeholders, including groups likely to push for maximum openness and accountability.
• The more visible a company or association, the more vulnerable it is to emerging strategies of global cyber-activism.	• Determine the leadership role the association will take in disclosing critical information and responding to public challenges.
• Transparency creates tremendous opportunity for global leadership on the issues that matter most to your members.	• Define the limits of transparency for your members and the association.
• Associations will be the forum for negotiating a new social contract between their members and the public.	• Train and equip your members and association to live in transparent world.
• The time to develop a transparency strategy is before a crisis hits.	

Transparency goes hand in glove with integrity. If you always take a position on merits, you need never fear public scrutiny.

— **Neil Offen, CAE**
President, Direct Selling Association

In democracies, citizens expect to be informed about what their leaders are doing, and elected officials have incentives (such as job security) to keep their constituents informed. Democratic societies develop attitudes and mores about transparency in the public sector that then shape expectations about behavior in the private and nonprofit sectors. Just consider: Will there someday be an association equivalent to the Freedom of Information Act?

Economic Globalization. In a global economy, investors want better information about the national economies and the companies in which they are placing their money. Countries under pressure to attract foreign investment demand information from both companies and government agencies. As trade, capital, pollution, crime, drugs, people, and ideas increasingly move on a global scale, those who are affected want information about what is happening—and they want to have a say. Investment analysts are already calling associations for information on industries and companies. Who else will be asking associations for vital economic information—and what questions will they ask?

The Digital Revolution. It would be hard to exaggerate the pace of the digital revolution and the globalization of digital technologies. Computing power has doubled roughly every 18 months for more than 25 years. Progress in telecommunications has become equally spectacular. Wireless phone service is expected to reach more than 2 billion people by 2010. The number of global Internet users is projected to grow from slightly over 400 million in 2000 to nearly 1.2 billion by 2005. Within a generation, wireless high-speed Internet access and videoconferencing will be available almost anywhere, and computerized translation will help reduce language barriers.

This expansion of connectivity enables people to easily communicate, seek and exchange information, and coordinate activities on a global scale. They can obtain information about corporations and governments, share that information, and coordinate social activism globally. What role might associations play in shaping the public perception pulsing through this global network?

When activists can send multiple messages with the click of a mouse, hundreds of Internet news groups can spring up overnight, and thousands of Web sites instantly proffer information and opinion, the traditional power of the media to focus public attention is amplified and far outstripped by an actively engaged public.

— Allen Hammond
Director of Strategic Analysis, World Resources Institute
Guest Expert, ASAE Foundation Futures Scan Community of Practice

The Rise of Transnational Civil Society. The plummeting cost of distributing information and organizing on a global scale has accelerated the development of transnational civil society—organized groups capable of imposing novel checks and balances on the power of every kind of organization. These nongovernmental organizations (NGOs) influence which issues receive attention; propose strategies for solving problems; and monitor the behavior of corporations, governments, and other organizations. Thousands of national NGOs and more than 15,000 transnational NGOs already exist. The growth of informal coalitions is outpacing the increase in formal organizations.

These civil society organizations are developing capabilities for global cyber-activism—linking themselves into transnational networks, coordinating their efforts globally for greater impact, and moving at Internet speed. All organizations of any significant size will potentially be under scrutiny by hundreds of NGOs and transnational networks around the world. For instance, the World Trade Organization and the World Bank are targets for activist groups taking issue with globalization.

Members will expect their associations to weigh in for their defense. And they will find associations to be the perfect forum to develop group norms around transparency. Yet as associations become those forums they, too, will be subject to scrutiny.

In the future, an association could easily be the target for an industry or issue. It might suffer damage to image and brand value, disappointment of major stakeholders, and loss of market share. The larger an organization is—and the more it has invested in its image or brand identity—the more vulnerable it is.

Transparency's Scope

The growing demands for transparency are broad ranging. The strongest demands are for information related to the bottom line—economic performance. But there are also demands for information about the "new bottom lines," which include the following:

FORMING GLOBAL ISSUES NETWORKS

Jean-Francois Rischard, vice president for Europe of the World Bank, argues that "the 19th century methods and glacial pace of global treaty-making and ratification" just don't cut it in dealing with 21st century global problems. The only approaches that have a chance, he believes, will be ones that share the network characteristics of the New Economy. They will be coalitions of associations, interested nations, private companies, and other non-governmental organizations. They will focus on setting standards or norms—much like the informal bodies that built out the Internet without treaties or legislated rules and regulations.

Rischard calls them *Global Issues Networks*. He hopes that, over time, they will issue ratings that measure how well countries and private businesses are doing in meeting specified norms on the environment and other issues that affect the welfare of the planet. The process will be quick and non-bureaucratic. The premise will be that if you don't meet the agreed-upon norms, you will be exposed as a rogue player in the global economy.

Reported by David Ignatius from the 2001 World Economic Forum in Davos, Switzerland

Economic Transparency. More mature market economies, such as the United States, have already developed fairly rigorous corporate disclosure standards. The pressure for standards has come from the marketplace itself. Financial markets can only function well when investors have the information they need to assess who will most productively use their capital. Now disclosure standards are coming into place to meet the demands of people investing internationally and of policy makers seeking to head off financial crises.

The more an economy is in flux, the less investors can rely on past reputations—and the more they need information. The inevitable economic churning caused by accelerating globalization, rapid technological change, and the growth of e-business will escalate demands for better information. As the Internet revolutionizes information access and allows investors and consumers to talk to each other, markets are insisting on ever-greater transparency.

We want access to your corporate information, to your plans and strategies, your best thinking, your genuine knowledge. We will not settle for the 4-color brochure, for Web sites chock-a-block with eye candy but lacking any substance...There are no secrets. The networked market knows more than companies do about their own products. And whether the news is good or bad, they tell everyone.

— **Rick Levine, et al.,** *The Cluetrain Manifesto*

Environmental Transparency. Home Depot, the world's largest lumber retailer, publicly committed itself to stop purchasing timber from endangered forests. The decision was largely the result of a transnational e-mail, Internet, and mass media campaign that exemplifies the emerging methods and capabilities of global cyber-activism. Although the Rain Forest Action Network and Greenpeace organized the campaign, it involved Internet coordination among hundreds of environmental organizations and grassroots groups around the world.

NGOs are also beginning to develop monitoring networks. For example, the World Resources Institute (WRI) is organizing Global Forest Watch, an international network of local forest protection groups linked by the Internet and a common data-gathering format. WRI collaborated by e-mail with more than 100 scientists worldwide to create a unique set of maps showing the location and extent of the world's old growth forests. Global Forest Watch monitors all these areas, recording on digital maps any illegal cutting, burning, or other violations of forest leases.

ARE YOU PREPARED?

Whether you are an association executive, a member, a supplier, or any other player in the association community, imagine that your organization is being subjected to the kind of reputation-threatening attacks that have been made against Royal Dutch/Shell, Nike, and many other organizations. What aspects of your organization's behavior could possibly draw such criticism, justified or not?

This information is posted on the Internet in near real-time, naming specific violators. Review processes check the accuracy of the data collected and ensure that participating network groups are acting responsibly. The information makes it possible for activists to mobilize quickly, apply market pressures to companies, and pressure governments to regulate effectively.

Government reporting requirements are another emerging strategy for promoting environmental transparency. With the passage of the Community Right to Know Act of 1986, the United States became the first country to mandate that companies emitting certain toxic chemicals must publicly report on those emissions. Other nations have followed suit.

NGOs often play a role here as well. In the United States, for example, the Environmental Defense Fund (EDF) posts the emissions data as an easy-to-understand environmental scorecard. People can go to the EDF Web site, type in their ZIP Codes, and find out to what degree industries in their areas are meeting EPA standards.

Social Transparency. In the late 1990s, when information circulated on the Internet showing that Nike produced some of its athletic shoes under unhealthy and exploitative working conditions, first CNN and then media outlets around the world picked up the story. Sales of Nike products plummeted. Within a few weeks, Philip Knight, Nike's founder and CEO, admitted, "The Nike product has become synonymous with slave wages, forced overtime, and arbitrary abuse." The company quickly instituted sweeping reforms to protect its brand value from permanent damage.

More sustained and systematic approaches are likely to arise as well. For example, Transparency International (TI) came into existence in 1993 and galvanized a global movement against corruption. TI's annual Corruption Perceptions Index ranks countries on how corrupt they are perceived, according to surveys of business leaders, political analysts, and the public. Ratings in TI's index often become headline news and the subject of legislative debates. TI is developing another index on which countries are home to corporations most likely to offer bribes. It is also building a combined local/global structure to help local chapters press their governments for reform.

Internal Transparency. As the external pressure for transparency grows, organizations will inevitably be pushed to be more transparent internally. Advocates of internal openness argue that secrecy and distrust sabotage efforts to empower employees and have them operate with a common purpose.

Inc. magazine coined the term "open book management" in a 1990 article on aspects of the movement toward greater internal transparency. This approach includes giving all employees regular feedback on how the organization is performing, involving employees in developing annual operating plans with target goals, and setting up incentive compensation programs that reward all employees in the same way as owners and senior managers.

In associations, *process transparency* enables members to see how to participate, get decisions made, and accomplish something. Associations with little process transparency risk limiting the involvement and motivation of newer members because only long-time members know how to operate. Process transparency also involves more openness about how decisions were made. Leadership by "command decision"—without explanation—is unacceptable to members who have a stake in the organization. Association leaders should have processes in place to track and explain how they arrived at important decisions.

Benefits and Limits

As pressures for transparency grow, association executives and boards need to consciously develop a "transparency strategy." That requires thinking through the full range of benefits of adopting a high-transparency strategy, while also considering their members' legitimate concerns.

Eventually, the truth will set us free. While it might make my job more difficult, in the long run transparency will benefit my association and most organizations.
— **Mark C. Anderson**
Executive Director, American Society for the Surgery of the Hand

An organization that adopts a principled, consistent policy of greater openness can gain several advantages.

A Trustworthy Reputation. Greater transparency in an organization creates a reputation for honesty and integrity and increases trust among all the parties who deal with it. If people believe an organization is operating with openness and honesty, they are more inclined to give the benefit of the doubt when problems arise. When there is a legitimate need to keep something private, people will be much more likely to accept that from an organization with an overall reputation for openness.

Higher Efficiency and Effectiveness. Operating in a transparent environment fosters better performance and accountability. It improves cooperation with affiliates, which sometimes assume that their parent organizations operate in secrecy. It reduces the need for and the likelihood of government involvement. Less energy is spent covering up mistakes, so time can be devoted to solving problems.

A Magnet for Membership. Transparency will draw in people—especially younger ones—who want to be a part of an open and honest organization. While older generations basically trust organizations, Gen X-ers are less likely to feel that way. The Millennial Generation, being raised on the Internet, expects open access to information.

Protection Against Hostile Attacks. Being more transparent sets a tone that fosters dialogue. Engaging critics in honest dialogue tends to diffuse hostile attacks and disruptive activities. An intentional transparency strategy can give an organization more control over the context in which information is presented, making it less likely that people will "take facts out of context" and attack actions out of misunderstanding.

Better Internal Learning. Transparency positively changes an organization's internal culture by encouraging more knowledge sharing. Without a culture of openness, people tend to build silos around their areas and keep information to themselves, which blocks both internal learning and transparency to the outside world.

Greater Social Contribution. Transparency helps an association more easily follow the high road. It helps ensure that the public interest, not just narrow self-interest, affects priority setting. More informed members and consumers are able to make wiser choices.

Despite these benefits, associations have legitimate concerns about the risks involved in moving toward greater transparency. Serious discussion and debate are justified within every association about how much transparency is enough, in view of these potential drawbacks:

Loss of Competitive Advantage. Organizations need to be able to protect information critical to maintaining their competitive edge, which is often created by knowledge others cannot easily replicate. Transparency should not require the disclosure of that knowledge.

Another common justification for managerial secrecy is to prevent others from taking advantage of information that may harm or distort the execution of a management plan during a specific time. For example, a veil of discretion is sometimes necessary when forming business partnerships, shifting alliances, and developing new business lines. Once the plan is implemented, however, the reasons for secrecy may no longer exist.

Unreasonable Critics. Not all NGOs, governments, and companies want to use information solely for the public good. Greater transparency can make an association (or its members) a better target for those who distort information and use it against the organization. Misinterpretation or deliberate misuse of information can spark unfavorable headlines or plunges in stock prices at member companies.

In such situations, withholding easily distorted information might be justified—but this rationale can lead to a return to secrecy. Delays in the release of information are certainly justifiable to check for accuracy and to make information harder to distort by presenting it "in context." Over time, developing a reputation for being open and trustworthy can make it easier to demonstrate that some critics are being unreasonable.

Privacy. Transparency does not apply in areas of "professional secrecy," such as attorney-client conversations and employment records. Transparency cannot be used as a rationale for revealing trade secrets, violating due process, or setting aside reasonable protections of personal privacy.

Lower Goals. Greater transparency could lead some associations and members to lower their goals, to avoid having people see where they fall short. This danger is not inevitable. Being open about a broad range of goals can make an association more aspiration-driven and thus more attractive to members seeking meaning.

Infoglut. Too much disclosure can cause "infoglut," making it hard to know what information is significant. Burying important information in a flood of data can even be a cynical strategy for preventing transparency. Transparency is not just a matter of making information public. It's a matter of releasing relevant information.

Decision Problems. Sunshine laws requiring open meetings can lead to a loss of candor among decision makers, a tendency to do everything with an eye to "how it looks," and an inhibition on brainstorming and creative speculation.

Member Readiness. Fears about the short-term problems and embarrassments of moving toward greater transparency may stop some members from being more open. As a result, association executives and boards are likely to find differences of opinion on this subject among their membership.

Partner Readiness. When operating in a coalition effort or a strategic alliance, some partners may not want to be as open about the joint activities as your own organization is willing to be. Protecting the integrity of co-created proprietary knowledge requires good communication between partners and may result in limits on transparency.

Developing a Strategy

More openness is not always better than less. Carrying any principle to its extreme can cause problems. The challenges in designing a transparency strategy are educating people about the benefits of openness and moving past people's resistance, while acknowledging (and respecting) well-grounded concerns about the disadvantages and limits of transparency.

It's not only the larger associations that have to be aware of transparency issues. Those of us from smaller associations without a public presence should be concerned about how open we are to our members and other audiences important to us, such as corporate partners, other associations with whom we work, and our industry press.

— Robin Kriegel, CAE
Executive Director, American Society for Parenteral and Eternal Nutrition

Developing a transparency strategy takes more than 15 minutes at a board meeting. In fact, years of effort might be necessary. These steps will help you get started:

- Start a process of discussion and study. Take your most progressive people, put them on a task force, and let them drive the issue.

- Identify and address legitimate concerns your members have about necessary "limits to transparency."

- Discuss transparency-related issues with stakeholders. Include public interest groups and government regulators in these conversations as appropriate.

- Frame an "Organizational Accountability Statement" that sets out your organization's philosophy on transparency and guidelines for behavior.

- Develop strategies for incorporating greater transparency into the internal culture and operations of your organization.

- Develop and conduct a Transparency Audit to identify important information that you do not share openly. Consider three levels of transparency: the public, members, and leadership and staff.

WHAT'S THE 990 OF THE FUTURE?

The Federal Form 990 annual information return is one standardized transparency requirement for associations. For many years, associations and other tax-exempt organizations were required to make certain parts of their Form 990 available for public inspection at their offices. Since 1999, tax-exempt organizations have been required to make their 990 tax returns "widely available to the public" or to provide photocopies to any person who requests them. "Widely available to the public" means putting the tax return (excluding certain donor information) on the World Wide Web. Putting your 990 on the Web changes its character from an obscure IRS form with numbers filled out by your finance officer to a public document that gives people a view into your association.

How could you improve your association's approach to completing Form 990 in order to increase your transparency and more thoughtfully frame the story you're telling about your association? What are some other areas on which you might have to provide regular reports? Can you provide some of that information now?

- Do a gap analysis of the information you do not share openly to assess whether secrecy is justified by the guidelines you developed in your accountability statement.

- Where your organization decides that organizational secrecy is justified, set out a clearly stated rationale and appropriate limits to the secrecy's time and scope.

- Develop your Web page as a transparent window into your organization. Post your strategic plan and other material that can help others understand your goals and the performance standards you have set.

- Create training events and programs for board members, staff, and members to improve skill sets for operating more transparently and for responding effectively to "bad news" events and charges against your organization, true or untrue.

- Reward staff members who identify ways to become more transparent internally and externally.

Transparency is an area of change where the light of associations can really shine and contribute to creating a better world. Because the association community includes a wide range of actors from across the economy and the professions, it can be an important agent in the evolution of a more transparent economy and society.

THE PATH TO TRANSPARENCY

Assume that several weeks ago you started a new position at the helm of leading national association. So far, it's been a fairly uneventful transition with no major crises. However, buried in the files, you found a folder of correspondence between your predecessor and a prominent industry manufacturer that discussed the possibility of an association product endorsement. The product endorsement plan is controversial for the association, and the agreement seems to have been reached without following proper oversight and vetting procedures. Few people are aware of the situation, but word could somehow leak out and both inflame and demoralize your membership.

You can sweep the incident under the carpet, and hope that nothing further will leak out—a fairly likely but not certain outcome. Or, you can proactively disclose the improper past practices of the association, renounce them, and publicly set new standards of behavior.

- What are the benefits and drawbacks of each approach?
- Is the risk of later involuntary revelation greater than the controversy that would come from immediate, deliberate disclosure?
- Would the adoption of a transparency approach change the likelihood of future problems?
- What is the downside of keeping quiet about the entire affair?
- What effect would each approach have on your efficacy as the new leader of the association?

Provocative Questions
For Association Executives and Leaders

Transparency involves operating in an open, accountable manner and providing the public with information it can use to evaluate your performance. Propelled by forces as powerful as the spread of democracy, economic globalization, the digital revolution, and the rise of transnational civil society, this is an issue to which all association leaders need to attend.

1. Associations can provide the forum for defining public expectations for performance on the new bottom lines. Which economic, social and environmental issues are relevant for your association? Why might good people in your association cross the line into unethical behavior related to keeping secrets and telling lies? To whom is your association accountable? Which stakeholders should participate in a transparency forum?

2. Process transparency is a key aspect of internal transparency. Can your members see how to participate, how decisions are made, how things get done, and how resources are allocated? Are your internal processes transparent to staff?

3. An organization that adopts a principled, consistent policy of greater openness can gain several advantages. How would transparency give you a trustworthy reputation? Higher efficiency and effectiveness? A magnet for membership? Protection against hostile attacks? Better internal learning?

4. Serious discussion and debate are justified within every association about how much transparency is enough. Would you lose competitive advantage? Increase your vulnerability to unreasonable critics? Invade legitimate zones of privacy? Lower your goals to easily achievable ones? Add to "infoglut"? Create decision problems? Push members and partners beyond their readiness?

5. Fully implementing a transparency strategy could require years of effort. Where is the urgency greatest for proceeding? What early steps could increase your association's readiness for transparency?

6. Associations will be a forum for negotiating a new social contract between their members and the public. How might transparency supersede public relations as an avenue to greater public understanding and collaboration?

Provocative Questions
For Business Partners

Businesses that want to work with associations will need to develop their own transparency strategy. Associations already conduct due diligence around performance when they decide to endorse products and services for their members. They choose services based on the values their members hold. In the future, businesses will be asked to disclose their economic, social, and environmental performance to close the deal. Here are just a few questions you might face in a transparency audit.

Economic

1. What financial information are you prepared to disclose to clients?

2. Can you offer assurance you will be in business to fulfill your commitment to the client?

3. Do have a way to share changes in financial condition with customers and clients?

4. Are there issues with your parent company, subsidiaries, or business alliances?

Social

1. What are your labor practices? Those of your suppliers?

2. Are you an equal opportunity business in word and deed?

3. Do you have a strong code of business ethics you follow throughout the world?

Environment

1. What impact does your business have on the environment?

2. Do you consider sustainability when you acquire resources to produce products and services?

3. Can you demonstrate a commitment to conservation through recycling, energy, and water use practices?

Recommended Resources

"Cyber-Activism: The Rise of Civil Accountability and It's Consequences for Governance," by Allen Hammond and Jonathan Lash in *Information Impacts*. Director of Strategic Analysis at the World Resources Institute argues that new forms of global "cyber-activism" are imposing checks and balances on the power of global corporations and are becoming an important part of global governance.

"Does the Invisible Hand Need a Transparent Glove?" by Ann Florini (Carnegie Endowment, 2000). Director of the Transparency Project at the Carnegie Endowment for International Peace examines why transparency is emerging as a major issue and addresses the advantages and disadvantages of relying on transparency to address global issues.

The Knowledge Executive: Leadership in an Information Society, by Harlan Cleveland (E.P. Dutton, 1985). This book by a former Associate Secretary of State and U.S. Ambassador to NATO remains one of the best guides to future-oriented leadership. One chapter argues that the benefits of greater openness are offset by risks of making it more difficult to get things done.

Open Book Management: The Coming Business Revolution, by John Case (HarperBusiness, 1996). The best of a large number of books published on open book management. Case shows, with many examples from open book companies, that organizations achieve major improvements in performance when they treat their employees like owners.

The Third Force: The Rise of Transnational Civil Society, edited by Ann Florini (Carnegie Endowment, 2000). The Third Force surveys transnational organizations and networks that are monitoring other institutions and influencing global policy-making. Case studies range from Transparency International and Amnesty International to the global movement to assess the costs and benefits of large dams.

When Good Companies Do Bad Things, by Peter Schwartz and Blair Gibb (John Wiley & Sons, 1999). Schwartz and Gibb present case studies of Royal Dutch/Shell, Nike, and many other companies that have had "bad behaviors" publicly exposed. They examine the companies' response strategies and the lessons of experience that emerge.

CHAPTER 7
Living Organizations

Living Organizations: Organizations that rely on self-organizing structures, purpose and values, trust, and knowledge sharing to adapt and evolve to meet emerging opportunities.

Whether their members are interested in apples or aircraft, baskets or bytes, children or chemicals, no association today is immune from the acceleration of change affecting society. The technologies on which their members' businesses and associations' own operations are based are changing constantly. They find themselves competing for resources, including time and talent. They face new competitors in the marketplace, as well as a "What have you done for me today?" mindset among members.

New partnerships and strategic alliances are the order of the day, as organizational identities link and blur. Uncertainty and change are becoming their only certainty.

In times of continuous change, there is an understandable tendency to increase control: Reengineer the organization; find a new leader to take command. But these machine-oriented metaphors, based on the industrial era, no longer resonate. Leading students of organizational change find more value in biological metaphors.

Associations are living systems in a real sense—they are not machines but groups of people working to create something together. Living systems have one enormous advantage over machines: They self-organize. There is no "boss" running ecological systems, yet they adapt and change continuously.

This new perspective suggests that instead of trying to control everything, association leaders need to view an organization as a living system with the ability to self-organize. To promote self-organization, leaders need to clarify their purpose and values, break down bureaucracy, and understand the importance of knowledge sharing and trust.

IMPLICATIONS FOR ASSOCIATIONS	ACTION STEPS
• Purpose and values provide the minimal instructions to self-organize without losing identity.	• Use dialogue to share beliefs, create commitment, and foster relationships.
• Living organizations run pilot projects, adopt any positive deviance, and learn from failures.	• Experiment with the next generation of knowledge communication technologies.
• Communities of practice are an emerging form of self-organization.	• Adopt association structures and processes that value positive deviance.
• Trust is the connective tissue holding a diverse system in collaboration.	• Apply the trust litmus test to check the health of your association.

Instead of trying to control everything in an environment of continuous change, association leaders must view their organizations as organic, self-organizing systems capable of constant adaptation and evolution.

— D. Brent Mulgrew
Executive Director, Ohio State Medical Association

Living organizations capable of adapting and thriving will use the power of self-organizing structures, as well as purpose and values, trust, and knowledge sharing.

Self-Organizing Structures

In the search for an optimum organizational structure, associations historically have focused on such issues as board governance, board–staff relationships, and organizational charts. In the 1990s, associations attempted to cope with rapidly changing environments through task forces and teams. Just as corporations flattened their hierarchies and fostered cross-functionality, associations tried to reengineer their way to greater speed and effectiveness. Proponents of total quality management, systems theory, and reengineering believed they could gain greater control and predictability by learning how to account for all the variables in the system and how those variables interact.

A STUDY IN CONTRASTS

Here is a side-by-side comparison of the characteristics found in traditional and living organizations:

TRADITIONAL	LIVING
Bylaws and Policies	Purpose and Values
Hierarchy	Networks and Adhocracy
Command and Control	Self-organization and Trust
Best Practices	Positive Deviance
Programs	Pilot Projects
Organizing to Do	Organizing to Learn and Do and Learn
Long-range Planning	Emergence
Briefings	Dialogue
Special Interest Groups	Communities of Practice
Divisions and Departments	Strategic Alliances

The world, however, is far more complex than any machine. Dynamic systems are a network of many agents freely choosing how to respond to multiple options. In a brain the agents are nerve cells; in an ecosystem the agents are species; in an economy the agents might be individuals or households. Adaptation is a continuous process of self-organization.

With the advent of network communications and inexpensive collaboration software, associations find it easier to coordinate complex interactions. Once communication technologies and basic instructions are in place, any business or association can be a hive of discrete yet interdependent strategic alliances. In the 20th century, associations were a good place to practice having effective meetings. In this century, they will be a great place to learn how to create self-organizing structures to work with anyone, anywhere.

LIVING ORGANIZATIONS IN ACTION

When Digital Addiction, the company sponsoring the computer game Sanctum, hit hard times, some of its 20,000 regular players were unwilling to give up the fun and relationships they had established. Their solution: they formed the Non-Profit International Online Gaming Association, bought the rights to the game, and set up a Web site. The association's board members are all unpaid volunteers, and meetings with members are held online. Instead of losing gamers, they now find they are receiving requests to program new games. If the organization makes more money than it needs to run the game, it gives the money to charity.

Leaders in self-organizing systems help weave a web of alliances and serve as the human connection between disparate structures. Leaders introduce people to one another, call them into affiliation around a common purpose, and later reconnect them in new alliances. In this role, leaders share knowledge, stories, and values to create a common culture and commitment.

Leaders find they, too, must continually adapt to cultivate their own potential within the self-organizing system. Their leadership practices need to reflect a convergence of styles and strategies matched to the momentum present. They must sense and respond, choosing competence in one encounter, relational power in another situation, or inspiration and empowerment with still another group. They understand that different settings evoke different qualities in both themselves and their followers.

TESTING THE LIMITS

This exercise will help board members or senior staff to accept the limits of their command and control over the association.

1. Ask the group to list the association functions over which it is important to exercise control.

2. Now, ask the group to strike from the list any function that is subject to unforeseen events or changes.

3. If your group is realistic, it will strike every item.

4. What are the implications for organizing work in the face of uncertainty?

THE POWER OF "GROUP FORMING NETWORKS"

Emerging "groupware" and "community tools" will radically increase the ease of forming groups to adapt to rapid change. Dr. David P. Reed, former vice president and chief scientist for Lotus Development Corporation, has developed the concept of Group Forming Networks to explain the power and flexibility of networked groups.

Network structures with robust lines of communication to facilitate the formation of smaller sub-groups can dramatically increase the possible combinations for action. In a small group with three people, it's possible to fashion only four different subgroup combinations. When you perform the same calculation for a network of 20 people, the number of potential groupings multiplies to 1,048,555. As more members enter a Group Forming Network, the number of potential subgroups rises exponentially. Of course, only a fraction of potential groups will ever form, but when dealing with exponential possibilities even fractions can accumulate rapidly.

Old network structures—such as the broadcast model—feed centralized information to network members with little opportunity for feedback. Newer network structures—such as the telephone model—allow network members to engage each other in transactional interactions. Emerging Group Forming Networks allow for sustained and continuing communications between any given network subgroup, which creates a fertile environment for synergistic interactions.

These new abilities to form associations offer opportunities. If the value of networks is greatest in the facilitation of spontaneous connections, then associations and their membership networks are positioned to mediate the exponential gains of a fully networked membership. On the other hand, the ease of group formation challenges associations to make their activities even more relevant to members who are free to turn elsewhere to meet their needs for affiliation.

Purpose and Values

Clear purpose allows people throughout an organization to work in alignment without having all their activities centrally controlled. Clear purpose also motivates people to form meaningful relationships while carrying out meaningful tasks. As many traditional association benefits become commodities that others can provide, members will increasingly evaluate associations according to the sense of meaning and purpose they bring to their lives.

Another factor will be the association's values. Members might choose a business organization committed to sustainable development, a health-care organization that promotes holistic medicine, or a faith-based voluntary service group. What associations do may be less important than what they *believe*, because changing conditions will require a reordering of services and strategies.

Associations have long recognized the necessity of defining their purpose or mission. Many have been less explicit about their core values. Yet the purpose and values enable associations to self-organize without losing their identity. They provide the framework to live in a world of multiplying options and internal freedom without getting lost. Together, purpose and values enable associations to move beyond command-and-control mission statements and action plans. They provide a centering force for spontaneously organizing complex human interactions around new opportunities.

How leaders behave will either reinforce or diminish the power of purpose and values within the social system. Because actions have always spoken louder than words, leaders must be vigilant in aligning their behavior with their stated values. Leaders should look for stories, events, and even simple routines that reinforce the organization's stated purpose and values. For example, an association that says it values work/life balance should schedule down time during its business meetings.

Strategic conversation is the best way to identify and communicate purpose and values. Individuals will respond to genuine opportunities to share their beliefs and renew their commitments to one another. Although a simple tactic, facilitating dialogue will grow in importance as a means of focusing fast-moving, self-organizing associations around a meaningful purpose.

Trust

Trust is built around people who understand each other and have a sense of shared history. They depend on common routines and language to speed routine processes through the community. They test their assumptions about new information and opportunities against the communal consciousness. They know when they can draw on their social capital to proceed—and when it would be better to confer. You've undoubtedly heard the expression, "trusting someone with your life." In a complex, adaptive organization, individuals indeed trust one another to preserve the life of the organization.

A SELF-ASSESSMENT OF TRUST

Using a 10-point scale, assess how much trust exists in your organization. The low end of the scale (1) means the communication cannot be trusted to be accurate, people cannot be trusted to be accountable, and so on. The high end (10) represents complete trust.

You might use this self-assessment as a prelude to a series of dialogues about boosting the trust level. Everyone has responsibility for adding to the trust that exists in the system. Frame the conversation in terms of the roles each individual can play in contributing to the health of your organization.

Communication 1...2...3...4...5...6...7...8...9...10

Decision Making 1...2...3...4...5...6...7...8...9...10

Risk Taking   1...2...3...4...5...6...7...8...9...10

Stewardship   1...2...3...4...5...6...7...8...9...10

Accountability 1...2...3...4...5...6...7...8...9...10

Leadership   1...2...3...4...5...6...7...8...9...10

Distrust paralyzes a living organization by shutting down open exchanges and interactions. People start sending through incomplete and misleading information to serve their own purposes. Dissension is high, and competing interests overwhelm any sense of common purpose. This condition, however, should not be confused with the chaos and energy of self-organization. Individuals in a self-organizing system must believe they benefit more from cooperation than competition. If they cannot find it within the current system, they will break away into a new environment and structures where trust can be reestablished.

Organizations are embodiments of the human desire to affiliate and be together, and that desire brings us face-to-face with complex, multiple dimensions of our existence. I often say that leadership is deeply personal and inherently collective. That's a paradox that effective leaders have to embrace. It does depend on them. It does depend on their convictions, their clarity, their personal commitment to their own cultivation. And on the other hand, it doesn't depend on them. It's an inherently collective phenomenon.

— Peter Senge
quoted in *Shambhala Sun,* January 2001

Contrast the typical association governance structure with the living organization. The former seeks approval, rather than empowerment, to act. Decision processes are slow and out of step with a changing world. They are designed to control for success, rather than to explore for emerging opportunities. Far too often only a few people are even aware of the issues at stake.

In contrast, living organizations are transparent and have dynamic communication channels for collecting knowledge and testing models. They know the goal of decision making is not only to make good immediate decisions but also learn how to make even better decisions in the future.

Traditional association governance is about establishing precedence: What do the bylaws or policies allow? Living organizations experiment and remember the lessons learned from failures for future reference. Traditional association boards go into shock during a crisis. Living organization boards have the resilience to adapt and respond.

Trust is the litmus test of a healthy living organization. In a self-organizing system, structure and decision processes can take many forms. Associations can make decisions in many ways in widely diverse situations, as long as their choices are adding rather than subtracting trust in their system. If trust is low, the purpose and values may not have sufficient strength to center the organization.

Because the power of purpose and values can only be proven through patterns of behavior, people in a living organization take the measure of their leaders to evaluate how much trust is in the system. When people measure the authenticity of a leader, they are evaluating whether he or she acts consistently with the organization's purpose and values.

Trust is hard to earn and easy to lose. Association leaders can nurture trust in their organizations by being the first to trust the motives and talents of their volunteers and staff. They have to believe that these specific people, at this specific opportunity, have all it takes to reach their vision of the future.

Knowledge Sharing

Associations invest heavily in providing education for their members. In a 1997 ASAE Foundation study, associations reported spending 18 percent of their total resources on educating and training their members. In the 1990s, education primarily focused on the transfer of best practices. The central question was what should members know, not how might they learn.

In the coming decade, associations will design their education systems to replicate the way living systems learn. Self-organizing systems are constantly developing models of how things work in their environment and refining those models through learning and adaptation. When they face a crisis, living systems do not retreat into tried and true routines. They move into "emergence," where the conditions favor creating something new, unexpected, and unpredicted.

Association leaders will become more adept at identifying the "positive deviance" in this state of emergence. Positive deviance is any unusual and unpredictable behavior that works and has reached sufficient stability to be reproduced over time throughout the system. In simple terms, these are the crazy ideas and pilot projects that prove to be better models for dealing with changing conditions. Leaders encourage these innovators to share their new models so that others can learn.

Associations must design their education systems to respect the learning that comes from failures as well as successes. Solutions from today's failures might match future conditions better. Just as a living system encodes all this knowledge for future reference and faster learning, associations will create the conditions to connect their members into dynamic learning.

Living organizations are literally nourished by this knowledge. They are communication intensive, with knowledge flowing through multiple

WHEN CAN A COMMUNITY OF PRACTICE BE USEFUL?

A task force orients itself around the task to be accomplished; a community of practice focuses on increasing everyone's capacity to learn. While you cannot create a community of practice, you can create the space to let one emerge.

Create a forum and resources for communities of practice when:

1. Your industry, profession, or cause faces a new challenge or opportunity. Your analysis will be much richer from the free flow of multiple perspectives.

2. Your association wants to be the leader in creating new knowledge on a topic or technique. The pioneers and innovators will appreciate having a forum to accelerate their individual learning. You can harvest their thinking and creativity, without burdening them with developing products and services.

3. New areas of specialization are developing. These practitioners have special interests that do not fit existing structures. New institutional structures might emerge once you can observe their explorations.

4. A controversial issue emerges. A community of practice is free to surface new ways of thinking about the issue, because it is not asked to recommend or decide a course of action.

Communities of practice will not succeed when:

1. You cannot be open to controversy and positive deviance. Since people freely join and freely share, they resist traditional institutional controls.

2. You do not see evidence of common interest and excitement. Communities of practice are self-forming and self-sustaining. When interest dies, individuals in the community move on.

channels in all directions within the system. Associations willing to lead in the experimentation with knowledge-sharing systems will have the advantage. These systems will find new forms in the creative tension between high tech and high touch. Future meetings will be designed for high interaction and experimentation, but people will continue to prefer face-to-face meetings.

People will become skilled in working within a community of practice, which is designed around knowledge, not prestige or power. Communities of practice are close-knit subsets of a larger organization that convene around common interests or challenges. They are self-organizing by definition. While a task force orients itself around the task to be accomplished, a community of practice focuses on increasing everyone's capacity to learn. Participants are not appointed; individuals convene a community of practice, and people elect to join.

Communities of practice develop their own language and ways of communicating. They can be face-to-face or online. They are not necessarily leaderless; someone usually emerges as the leader, guide, and facilitator. People gain stature in the community according to their willingness to share knowledge and the quality of their contributions. Communities of practice die when control becomes too great; however, they need some structure to facilitate learning.

Associations will become more adept at proposing structure and processes to connect these communities, as well as wiser about the tensions that positive deviance creates in the established system.

Leading the Way

As the people most open to positive deviance and most willing to champion new learning, association leaders will become the master learners in these communities of practice. The measure of their power in a learning society will be their ability to create conditions favoring experimentation. They will make failure a socially acceptable option, especially if the failure comes trying to do something remarkable. They will be the ones seeding organizational conversations with stories about what people have tried, rather than what they have accomplished. The stories leaders tell about their own experimentation and learning will encourage people to try new and untested ideas and projects.

If there is a new sixth sense for leaders, it is being able to interpret "emergence" to their organizations—to spot good ideas, worthwhile activities, and useful structures that are emerging and to nurture these developments and lend their credibility to what others have discovered. Leaders clear the way and provide the resources for these new forms to be created; they also are the first to share new learning throughout the system.

Saying a leader is "in the know" will refer to more than knowing what has happened. It will mean the leader understands what is emerging.

TAPPI's Journey

Founded in 1915, TAPPI has grown into the world's largest professional association serving the pulp, paper, and converting industries. Its 28,500 individual members look to the association for information, education, and knowledge-sharing opportunities. In its 2010 Vision, TAPPI has started the journey to becoming an exemplar of the living organization.

TAPPI has 11 transition teams working to transform the association according to its vision, which is outlined below. The scope of two task forces speak directly to the principles of self-organizing: the Bureaucracy Busters and the Community Development transition teams. (For more information on TAPPI's 2010 Vision, visit www.tappi.org.)

WHAT IS 2010?

An effort to make TAPPI a more nimble and responsive organization.

Key Elements of the 2010 Vision

TAPPI members will have the opportunity to be involved in member communities that:

- Are easy to participate in
- Deliver high value to those involved
- Operate with minimal rules and maximum flexibility
- Are free from cumbersome structures and processes
- Are easy to form as new needs arise
- Products, services, information and staff competencies that are aligned to industry needs
- A more responsive association that can move more quickly to meet their needs

Why Are Changes Being Made?

TAPPI is a good organization that wants to become great organization. It is changing to stay relevant to meet changing needs of the members and the industries served.

What Is Not Changing?

TAPPI's core purpose and values:

Vision: to be a dynamic global community of individuals committed to the development and application of technology in the paper and related industries.

Core Purpose: To contribute to the industry's success by advancing technical and professional achievement of individuals in our global community.

Core Values: Individual growth, continuous improvement, integrity and fellowship, service to the industry.

TAPPI will continue to focus on what brings value to members:

- Access to technical information and experts, including peer interaction
- Content that is directly and immediately relevant
- Immediate accessibility, often online
- Industry information and news

Bureaucracy Busters Transition Team Scope

- Identify processes, policies, or procedures that work well and can be used as excellent models for the future
- Identify and eliminate real or perceived bureaucracy
- Act as sounding board for recommendations of simplified processes, policies, or procedures to replace the bureaucratic ones while ensuring that the information needs of the users are met
- Re-engineer staff and volunteer interfaces
- Liaison with the Communications Team to inform constituencies of progress

Community Development Transition Team Scope

Promote and facilitate the formation of communities and provide nurturing in the early stages:

- Outside the existing Division/Local Section and committee structures
- Between Divisions and committees
- In geographic areas where members with common interests are clustered
- On topics that don't have a logical home in an existing community.

LETTER TO A FUTURE GENERATION

Objective: To explore heartfelt personal aspirations for your association.

Time Requirements: 45 minutes

Number of People: 6–12 people per group; the workshop breaks up into small discussion groups for this exercise.

Material Requirements: A pad of paper and pencil or pen for each participant. At least one flip chart pad, and three or four markers per small group; masking tape.

Setup: Best done with participants sitting around a table. In the first part of the exercise, each participant will be writing his or her own "Letter to a Future Generation." In the second part, split the participants into pairs and have them share their letters. Encourage them to take notes on what they find moving and inspiring in their partner's letter.

Potential Problems: This is often a deeply moving exercise because it puts people in contact with their hearts as well as their heads. During the part of the exercise when people share their letters in pairs, people who get deeply involved in their discussion may lose track of time. Give the group "time warnings" and announce when it is time to stop discussing one person's letter and shift to the other person's. Be sensitive to the state of the group. If animated discussions are underway, give the discussion a little more time.

Think of the "Letter to a Future Generation" as a personal statement to a younger generation, such as a grandchild or young person you are mentoring. It helps to imagine you are in the future, at the end of a long, fulfilling career, leaving behind important words. In the letter, express what you would want this young person to remember you for and what you did to help make the world better. *Go beyond things you and your association have already accomplished.* Emphasize your hopes for what you can accomplish in the future, writing the letter as if those hopes have come true.

Each participant should take 10 minutes to write an individual letter. Next the groups should be divided into pairs. One person in each pair reads the letter they have written while the other person listens intently and takes notes on thoughts or phrases that seem most inspiring, meaningful, moving, or important. Listeners can ask questions to clarify the meaning of statements in the letter and to draw out further information. After about 7 minutes, shift so that the people who have been listening now get to read and discuss their letters while the other people take notes.

After both people in the pairs have shared their letter with each other, the small group should come back together for 15 minutes to discuss the results. Each person in the group speaks as a "listener," reporting on what their partner said. The recorder takes notes on the conversation on the flip chart. When this sharing is completed, work together to identify a few ideas or phrases that struck everyone as especially inspiring, meaningful, moving, or important.

Take about 15 minutes for a full group discussion where the small groups briefly report their results and everyone reflects on the ideas and phrases that seem most inspiring and important. These are candidates for your association's purpose and values.

Provocative Questions
For Association Executives and Leaders

Associations are living systems in a real sense—they are not machines but groups of people working to create something together. This new perspective suggests that instead of trying to control everything, association leaders need to view an organization as a living system with the ability to self-organize.

1. Associations who see themselves as living systems appreciate that change is constant and necessary. They ask: Who are we becoming? What kind of leaders do we need to become this?

2. Living organizations use minimal instructions to self-organize in response to emerging reality. Does your association have a set of minimal instructions it can use in responding to future possibilities?

3. With the advent of network communications and collaboration software, associations can work with any number of individuals in any location for any period of time. What investment has your association made in new ways of working together? How are traditional participation processes being transformed?

4. Leaders in self-organizing systems will be the weavers of a web of alliances. How connected are your leaders? Is anyone critical outside the leader's web?

5. Purpose and values are the simple instructions that enable associations to self-organize without losing their identity. Does your association have a sufficient framework to live in a world of intense options?

6. Leaders must be able to facilitate dialogue. How can you help your leaders transform from "my way" to "our way"?

7. Trust is the litmus test of a healthy living organization. What is your association doing to add trust to its system? How are you subtracting trust?

8. Association leaders will become more adept at identifying the positive deviance—any unusual and unpredictable behavior that is working. How does your association welcome what is learned outside its normal channels?

9. If there is a new sixth sense for leaders, it is being able to interpret emergence to their organizations. Are your leaders operating as master learners and embracing their role as guides in a changing environment?

10. Command and control is over. How ready is your association to become a living organization with self-organizing structure held together by purpose and values, trust, and knowledge?

Provocative Questions
For Business Partners

The businesses serving associations will find the best way to work with self-organizing associations is to become self-organizing themselves. Here are some additional implications of doing business with living organizations:

1. If decision making is distributed throughout the organization, the person who has formal authority may not have actual authority over the decision to buy your products or services. How do you connect to the real decision makers?

2. If relationships are key to repeat business, how do you maintain contact with people who are in constantly shifting roles and structures?

3. Self-organizing systems make greater use of strategic alliances. Whose web of alliances are you in now and whose would you like to join? Is there any competitive overlap or have those old rules faded away?

4. If associations become more spontaneous, will you have the rapid-response time to meet their needs?

5. Volunteers may have greater resources at their disposal to support their self-organizing activities. How do you sell to these new buyers?

6. Associations placing a premium on trust will not suffer broken promises well. How prepared are you to deliver what you promise?

Recommended Resources

Birth of the Chaordic Age, by Dee Hock (Berrett-Keohler, 1999). A lively autobiography of the leader behind creating VISA International. He shows how organizations can blend chaos and order to produce success.

The Connective Edge, Leading in an Interdependent World, by Jean Lipman-Blumen (Jossey-Bass, 1996). Connective leaders use themselves and everything around them as instruments to their goals.

E-Volve, Succeeding in the Digital Culture of Tomorrow, by Rosabeth Moss Kanter (Harvard Business School, 2001). A carefully researched study of online businesses that provides solid principles and insights for any organization competing in a networked world.

Leadership and the New Science, by Margaret J. Wheatley (Berrett-Keohler, 2001). A layman's introduction to how nature creates infinite diversity and how these scientific principles can be applied to leading human organizations.

Surfing the Edge of Chaos, The Laws of Nature and the New Laws of Business, by Richard T. Pascale, Mark Millemann, and Linda Gioja (Crown, 2000). A practical book about the parallels between business and nature that offers a bold new way of thinking about strategic challenges in business.

Conclusion: Becoming a 2010 Association

Opportunities are never lost; they are taken by others.
—**Source Unknown**

What will your association be like in 2010? You can begin to develop possible answers to this question by starting strategic conversations about the potential the future offers. Explore any of the seven issues, and you will realize just how many profound options—and therefore, choices—you have within each concept. If you have any doubt about how varied your options are, take time to discuss a few of the provocative questions with your board, committees, and staff.

The future is sure to be both uncertain and demanding. Your organization will thrive if you base your explorations on an enduring meaning that transcends time and individual interests. Keep returning to the idea that "meaning matters most," and you will not lose your way. In 2010, your association must be able to say, "Our members care about what we are doing, and they want to be involved in the effort."

But what about these provocative questions? It's often tempting to look for quick, air-tight answers. But you cannot decode the future like a true–false exam on life. You can only learn as you go: ask the tough questions, postulate possible answers, experiment with choices, regroup after setbacks, and continually construct and reconstruct new models that make sense of and for your world. Doing well in 2010 depends on becoming a learning culture today; learning how to learn in new ways may well be the first step.

The future is not within your command and neither are the people that will inhabit it. Accepting your association as a living organization will free you to adapt in all the ways the future will require. Trust what can emerge in your association when you support your members and staff; make it possible for them to move toward a clear and good purpose by keeping the larger goals visible and compelling and letting the details take care of themselves.

What is emerging in the association community directly parallels what is emerging in society. The simple definition of an association has always been (and always will be) "people working together for a common purpose." The successful association of 2010 will be much smarter about the people side of its business. Associations expecting to fit people into fixed, predetermined molds will fail. But associations that shape themselves around the rich differences among people, including their generational experiences, will find they can successfully leverage the extraordinary human resources of creativity and commitment. Inclusivity opens the way to synergy and greater organizational capacity.

Your association is operating in a world that is increasingly a smaller, more intimate place in which to accomplish the biggest things you can imagine. This is the promise of glocalization. The most effective associations in 2010 will have a world vision that sees connections everywhere, beyond the artificial boundaries of time, geography, and tradition. Responding to individual needs on a global scale can be a daunting but liberating goal, and enabling each individual to have a global reach is similarly remarkable.

The world will be looking at associations with ever-greater scrutiny in the years ahead. This is why transparency is not an optional issue in this list of seven. By 2010 some associations, companies, industries and professions will have stumbled badly in the choices they made. Transparency doesn't imply living perfect, squeaky-clean lives. It means having an attitude of accountability that invites inquiry, understanding, acceptance and forgiveness.

These seven emerging opportunities will not be the only ones your association will face between now and 2010; some old ones may re-emerge, and some new ones might arise. However, these seven can be profound places to begin exploring what your association could become.

It takes only one really important idea to launch a transformation. You now have at least seven. Get busy—the future begins tomorrow.

Appendix A
Resources for Further Exploration

The 7 Habits of Highly Effective People: Powerful Lessons in Personal Change, by Stephen R. Covey (Fireside, 1990).

Adult Learning in Associations: Models for Good Practice, by Clifford Baden (ASAE Foundation, 1997).

Age Power: How the 21st Century Will Be Ruled by the New Old, by Ken Dychtwald (JP Tarcher, 1999).

Aha! 10 Ways to Free Your Creative Spirit and Find Your Great Ideas, by Jordan Ayan (Crown, 1997).

American Generations: Who They Are. How They Live. What They Think, by Susan Mitchell (New Strategist, 1998).

Art of the Long View: Planning for the Future in an Uncertain World, by Peter Schwartz (Doubleday, 1992).

Associations and Global Marketplace: Profiles in Success, by Kimberly Svevo-Cianci (American Society of Association Executives, 1995).

Becoming Virtual, by Pierre Levy and Robert Bononno (Plenum Trade, 1998).

Birth of the Chaordic Age, by Dee Hock (Berrett-Keohler, 1999).

Blur: The Speed of Change in the Connected Economy, by Stan Davis and Christopher Meyer (Warner Books, Inc., 1998).

Bowling Alone, by Robert D. Putnam (Simon & Schuster, 2000).

Building a House for Diversity: How a Fable About a Giraffe & an Elephant Offers New Strategies for Today's Workforce, by R. Roosevelt Thomas, Jr., and Marjorie I. Woodruff (AMACOM, 1999).

Building a Knowledge-Based Culture: Using Twenty-first Century Work and Decision-Making Systems in Associations, by Glenn H. Tecker, Kermit M. Eide, and Jean S. Frankel (ASAE Foundation, 1997).

Building Wealth, by Lester C. Thurow (HarperCollins, 1999).

Built to Last: Successful Habits of Visionary Companies, by James Collins and Jerry Porras (Harpercollins, 1994).

Business @ the Speed of Thought, by Bill Gates (Warner Books, 1999).

Changing by Design, by Douglas C. Eadie (Jossey-Bass, 1997).

The Cluetrain Manifesto: The End of Business as Usual, by Rick Levine, et al. (Perseus, 2000).

Community as Strategy: Creating the "Stickiness" of Community—Ten Fundamentals (www.asaenet.org/foundation).

Community as Strategy: People Make it Work: The Social Fabric of Community on the Web (www.asaenet.org/foundation).

The Community of the Future, edited by Frances Hesselbein, et al. (Jossey-Bass, 1998).

Competing for the Future, by Gary Hamel and C. K. Prahalad (Harvard Business School Press, 1994).

The Connective Edge, Leading in an Interdependent World, by Jean Lipman-Blumen (Jossey-Bass, 1996).

Creating a New Civilization, by Alvin Toffler and Heidi Toffler (Bantam Books, 1994).

Creating Value in the Network Economy, by Don Tapscott (Harvard Business School Press, 1999).

Cultural Creatives: How 50 Million People are Changing the World, by Paul Ray and Sherry Ruth Anderson (Harmony, 2000).

Cultural Diversity in the United States: A Critical Reader, edited by Ida Susser and Thomas C. Patterson (Blackwell, 2001).

Digital Darwinism, by Evan I. Schwartz (Broadway Books, 1999).

The Diversity Directive: Why Some Initiatives Fail & What to do About It, by Robert Hayles and Armida Mendez Russell (McGraw-Hill, 1997).

Diversity Success Strategies, by Norma Carr-Ruffino (Butterworth-Heinemann, 1999).

The Diversity Toolkit: How You Can Build and Benefit from a Diverse Workforce, by William Sonnenschein (Contemporary Books, 1999).

The Dream Society, by Rolf Jensen (McGraw-Hill, 1999).

Economy of Icons: How Businesses Manufactured Meaning, by Ernest Sternberg (Praeger, 1999).

Embracing the Future: An Action Guide for Association Leaders, by Rhea L. Blanken and Allen Liff (ASAE Foundation, 1999).

E-Volve, Succeeding in the Digital Culture of Tomorrow, by Rosabeth Moss Kanter (Harvard Business School, 2001).

The Experience Economy, by Joseph B. Pine and James Gilmore (Harvard Business School Press, 1999).

Facing the Future: A Report on the Major Trends and Issues Affecting Associations, by ASAE Foundation (ASAE Foundation, 1999).

The Female Advantage: Women's Ways of Leadership, by Sally Helgesen (Doubleday, 1995).

The Fifth Discipline Fieldbook: Strategies and Tools for Building a Learning Organization, edited by Peter Senge and Art Kleiner (Currency Doubleday, 1994).

The Fifth Discipline: The Art and Practice of the Learning Organziation, by Peter Senge (Doubleday, 1994).

The Fourth Turning, by Neil Howe and William Strauss (Broadway, 1998).

The Fourth Wave: Business in the 21st Century, by Herman B. Maynard and Susan E. Mehrtens (Berrett-Koehler, 1993).

The Future and Its Enemies, by Virginia Postrel (Free Press, 1998).

Future of the Self: Inventing the Postmodern Person, by Walter Truett Anderson (Tarcher, 1998).

A Future Perfect: The Challenge and Hidden Promise of Globalization, by John Micklethwait and Adrian Wooldridge (Times, 2000).

Future Talk: Conversations About Tomorrow With Today's Most Provocative Personalities, by Larry King and Pat Piper (HarperCollins, 1999).

Generation 2K, by Wendy Murray Zoba (Intervarsity, 1999).

Generation X: The Young Adult Market, by Susan Mitchell (New Strategist, 1997).

Generations at Work, by Ron Zemke, Claire Raines, and Bob Filipczak (AMACOM, 1999).

Global Civil Society: Dimensions for the Nonprofit Sector, by Lester Salamon, et al. (Johns Hopkins University Press, 1999).

The Global Forum of Societies of Association Executives. A network for the professional association executive community worldwide (www.asaenet.org/globalforum).

Global Literacies: Lessons on Business Leadership and National Cultures, by Robert Rosen, et al. (Simon & Schuster, 2000).

Globalization and the Challenges of the New Century: A Reader, edited by Patrick O'Meara and Howard D. Mehlinger (Indiana University Press, 2000).

Going Global: An Association Primer, ASAE Background Kit (American Society of Association Executives, 2000).

Going Local: Creating Self-Reliant Communities in a Global Age, by Michael H. Shuman (Free Press, 1998).

The Great Disruption, by Francis Fukuyama (Free Press, 1999).

Growing Up Digital: The Rise of the Net Generation, by Don Tapscott (McGraw-Hill, 1998).

Implementing Diversity, by Marilyn Loden (McGraw-Hill, 1996).

Jamming: The Art and Discipline of Business Creativity, by John Kao (HarperBusiness, 1997).

Joining Together, Group Theory and Group Skills, by David W. Johnson and Frank P. Johnson (1997).

Keeping Members: CEO Strategies for 21st Century Success, by Arlene Farber Sirken and Michael P. McDermott (ASAE Foundation, 1995).

The Leader of the Future: New Visions, Strategies, and Practices for the Next Era, edited by Frances Hesselbein (Jossey-Bass, 1997).

Leader to Leader: Enduring Insights on Leadership from the Drucker Foundation's Award-Winning Journal, by Frances Hesselbein and Paul M. Cohen (Jossey-Bass, 1999).

Leadership and the New Science, by Margaret J. Wheatley (Berrett-Keohler, 2001).

The Lexus and the Olive Tree: Understanding Globalization, by Thomas Friedman (Anchor, 1999).

Man's Search for Meaning, by Viktor E. Frankl (1984).

Management Challenges for the 21st Century, by Peter F. Drucker (HarperBusiness, 1999).

A Manager's Guide to Globalization: Six Skills for Success in a Changing World, by Stephen H. Rhinesmith (Irwin, 1996).

Managing Your Future as an Association, Thinking about Trends and Working Their Consequences, by Jennifer Jarratt, Joseph Coates, John B. Mahaffie, and Andy Hines (ASAE Foundation, 1994).

Millennials Rising: The Next Great Generation, by Neil Howe and William Strauss (Vintage, 2000).

Millennium Membership: How to Attract and Keep Members in the Workplace, by Mark Levin (American Society of Association Executives, 1999).

Net Future: The 7 Cyber Trends That Will Drive Business, Create New Wealth, and Define Your Future, by Chuck Martin (McGraw-Hill, 1999).

Net Worth, by J. Hagel and Marc Singer (Harvard Business School Press, 1999).

New Rules for the New Economy, by Kevin Kelly (Penguin Group, 1998).

On Leadership, by John W. Gardner (Free Press, 1993).

One to One Fieldbook, by Don Peppers, Martha Rogers, and Bob Dorf (Bantam, 1999).

The One to One Future: Building Relationships One Customer at a Time, by Don Peppers and Martha Rogers (Doubleday, 1997).

Open Book Management: The Coming Business Revolution, by John Case (HarperBusiness, 1996).

Organization of the Future (Drucker Foundation Future Series), edited by Frances Hesselbein, et al. (Jossey-Bass, 1997).

A Peacock in the Land of Penguins: A Tale of Diversity and Discovery, by Barbara Hateley and Warren H. Schmidt (Berrett-Koehler, 1997).

Power of Purpose: Creating Meaning in Your Life and Work, by Richard J. Leider (Berrett-Keohler, 1997).

Redefining Diversity, by R. Roosevelt Thomas, Jr. (AMACOM, 1996).

Release 2.1 by Esther Dyson (Broadway Books, 1998) .

Riding the Waves of Culture: Understanding Cultural Diversity in Global Business, by Fons Trompenaars and Charles Hampden-Turner (McGraw-Hill, 1998).

The Roaring 2000s, by Harry S. Dent (Simon & Schuster, 1998).

Rocking the Ages: The Yankelovich Report on Generational Marketing, by Walker Smith and Ann Clurman (HarperBusiness, 1997).

The Search for a New Beginning: Developing a New Civilization, by Mikhail Gorbachev (Harpercollins, 1995).

Self-Renewal: The Individual and the Innovative Society, by John W. Gardner (1995).

Serious Play: How the World's Best Companies Simulate to Innovate, by Michael Schrage (Harvard Business School, 2000).

The Social Life of Information, by John Seely Brown and Paul Duguid (Harvard Business School, 2000).

Surfing the Edge of Chaos: The Laws of Nature and the New Laws of Business, by Richard T. Pascale, Mark Millemann, and Linda Gioja (Crown, 2000).

The Third Force: The Rise of Transnational Civil Society, edited by Ann Florini (Carnegie Endowment, 2000).

The Xers & the Boomers: From Adversaries to Allies, by Claire Raines (Crisp, 2000).

Third Wave, by Alvin Toffler (Bantam Books, 1991).

When Good Companies Do Bad Things, by Peter Schwartz and Blair Gibb (John Wiley & Sons, 1999).

Which World? Scenarios for the 21st Century, by Allen Hammond (Island Press, 1998).

Working With Emotional Intelligence, by Daniel P. Goleman (Doubleday, 2000).

Research Tools on the Web
Customized News Retrieval and Tracking Services

The Internet has given birth to several powerful and convenient news retrieval services. These enable you to track news wires and publications for the latest news on specific topics, companies, or people.

Dow Jones Interactive at http://djinteractive.com

Inquisit at http://www.inquisit.com

Lexis-Nexis at http://www.lexis-nexis.com

Newspage at http://www.newspage.com

Pointcast at http://www.pointcast.com

Reuters Business Briefing at http://www.reuters.com/rbb

Online Reference Services

CNBC/Dow Jones (http://www.cnbcdowjones.com). Live and archived video, audio, and multimedia clips of press conferences and corporate presentations.

The Electric Library (http://www.elibrary.com). Subscribers can launch a comprehensive, simultaneous search through more than 150 full-text newspapers, hundreds of full-text magazines, two international news wires, two thousand classic books, hundreds of maps, thousands of photographs, as well as major works of literature and art.

Northern Light (http://www.northernlight.com). A combination research service and search engine.

Resources for Navigating the Web

ASAE Internet Resource Links at http://www.asaenet.org/InformationCentral/ICResmap.html.

Library of Congress at http://lcweb.loc.gov and the Library of Congress Guide to Internet Resources at http://lcweb.loc.gov/global/explore.html.

CEO Express at www.ceoexpress.com. A directory of links to major newspapers and trade magazines, custom news feeds, and government agencies.

Search Engines/Portals

Altavista at http://www.altavista.com

Deja News at http://www.dejanews.com

Excite at http://www.excite.com

Go2Net at http://www.go2net.com

Google at http://www.google.com

Hotbot at http://www.hotbot.com

Links2Go at http://www.links2go.com

Lycos at http://lycos.com

The Mining Company at http://home.miningco.com

Yahoo at http://yahoo.com

Future-Focused Web Sites

Coates & Jarratt at http://www.coatesandjarratt.com. (In particular, see the site's Futures Resources and Other Links at http://www.coatesand-jarratt.com/resources.html.)

Environmental Scanning Program of the University of Georgia Center for Continuing Education newsletter at http://www.gactr.uga.edu/scanning/lookouts.html.

Diversity Web Sites
www.amid.org
The American Institute for Managing Diversity's Web page features profiles in diversity, its Diversity Leadership Academy, research, education, a diversity store, Internet resources, and publications.

www.att.com/learningnetwork/diversity/
The AT&T learning network on the Web has diversity resources, lists of national organizations and programs, teaching cross-cultural awareness resources, and teaching tolerance resources.

www.cob.ohio-state.edu/~diversity/
The Fisher College of Business, Ohio State University, has a Teaching Diversity Resources List. This list of writings addresses diversity issues as they relate to various aspects of business and employment. Some are excellent cases to use in training and discussion.

www.latino.sscnet.ucla.edu/diversity/
This is a guide to special diversity resources for African American, Asian American, Latinos, Native American, multicultural, women, and gay and lesbian services on the Internet. Includes a list of multicultural associations, universities, reports, information, newsgroups, national organizations, and electronic resources.

www.nadm.org
The National Association for Diversity Management Web site lists online resources of Web sites, trainers and consultants, databases and

archives, diversity publications, statistics and surveys, life and family issues, frequently asked questions, training and curriculum, conferences, books, human resources, healthcare, public sector, and social services.

Government Research

The Library of Congress Web site provides the following gateway links:

- Executive Branch at http://lcweb.loc.gov/global/executive/fed.html

- Legislative Branch at http://lcweb.loc.gov/global/legislative/congress.html

- Judicial Branch at http://lcweb.loc.gov/global/judiciary.html

- State and local governments at http://lcweb.loc.gov/global/state/stategov.html

Federal Information Center (FIC) at http://fic.info.gov. Established in 1966, FIC is a single point of contact for people who have questions about federal agencies, programs, and services.

Fedworld Information Services at http://www.fedworld.gov. This service is maintained by the U.S. Department of Commerce.

Search government Web sites at http://www.nwbuildnet.com/nwbn/gov_search.html.

Statistics from more than 70 government agencies at http://www.fedstats.gov.

Thomas Legislative Information on the Internet at http://thomas.loc.gov/home/thomas2.html.

Magazines, Journals, and Newsletters
Getting Started—How to Locate Publications

Need to find publications in any topic area? Use these resources to help you locate publications:

http://pub.savvy.com. A comprehensive list of topics and more than 11,000 newsletters.

http://www.ceoexpress.com. Provides a good list of magazines and online publications.

http://www.enews.com. Electronic Newstand provides access to popular magazine subscriptions.

http://www.ajr.newslink.org. *American Journalism Review* Newslink provides access to newspapers and magazines.

http://www.owt.com/dircon/mediajum.htm. The US All Media Jumpstation features Direct Contact Publishing's comprehensive media guide to more than 3,000 magazines, professional journals, and trade and consumer publications. Strong on trade publications and professional journals.

http://www.rowe.com. Enables you to find thousands of publications—search by title or keywords—and subscribe online.

The Changing Business Environment

Fast Company. Seeks out examples of innovative companies and the people who lead them (http://www.fastcompany.com/home.html).

Wired. Looks at new ways of doing business—has a strong technology perspective (http://www.wired.com).

Fortune (http://www.fortune.com).

Demographics

American Demographics. Tracks demographic and consumer trends and is written for business executives (phone: 800/350-3060; Web site: http://www.demographics.com).

Census and You. This monthly publication is by the U.S. Census Bureau (contact: U.S. Government Printing Office at 202/512-1800 or on the Web at http://www.gpo.gov).

Population Today. This is the publication of the Population Reference Bureau, Washington, D.C. (download free copies at http://www.prb.org/poptoday.htm).

The Statistical Abstract of the United States. A useful selection of population data (contact: Government Printing Office at 202/512-1800 or on the Web at http://www.gpo.gov).

Future-Oriented Publications

Forecast, published by American Demographics, is a newsletter of demographic trends and business forecasts (phone: 1-800/350-3060; Web site: www.demographics.com).

The Trends Journal, a quarterly newsletter, distills the voluminous ongoing research of the Trends Research Institute of Rhinebeck, New York. The Institute tracks 300 separately defined domestic and international trend categories, including business, economics, politics, social developments, education, health, science, technology, philosophy, the arts, entertainment, and fashion (phone: 914/876-6700; Web site: http://www.trendsresearch.com).

The Worlds Future Society (phone: 1-800/989-8274; Web site: http://www.wfs.org/wfs/index.htm) publishes:

- *The Futurist.* A monthly magazine of forecasts, trends, and ideas about the future; subscription is included in its membership fee.

- *Future Survey.* A monthly digest abstracting scores of future-oriented books, articles, and reports. Future Survey provides user-friendly abstracts of new books, articles, and reports on topics that may have a major impact on the future. It points to the cutting-edge thinking of social critics, think-tank analysts, academic experts, and visionaries.

- *Futures Research Quarterly.* A scholarly journal for the professional futurist.

General Sources

The New York Times (http://www.nytimes.com)

Time (http://www.time.com)

Vital Speeches of the Day. Collects and reprints a selection of interesting and significant speeches made by leaders in business, government, education, the nonprofit sector, and many other fields. City News Publishing Company (phone: 843/881-8733).

The Wall Street Journal (http://interactive.wsj.com)

Globalization

The Asian Wall Street Journal. Covers developments in Asia (http://www.awsj.com).

The Economist. Published weekly, covers international affairs, business, science, and technology (http://www.economist.com).

The Financial Times. A weekday newspaper that monitors developments in international business and government (http://www.ft.com).

Social Change

The Gallup Poll. A monthly magazine of the Gallup organization (http://www.gallup.com/The_Poll/thepoll.asp).

The Monthly Labor Review. A publication by the Bureau of Labor Statistics (http://stats.bls.gov), U.S. Department of Labor. Discusses workplace issues and statistics on the workforce, including projections. The online version can be accessed at http://stats.bls.gov/opub/mlr/mlrhome.htm. To subscribe to the print version, contact the Government Printing Office at 202/512-1800 or on the Web at http://www.gpo.gov.

The Social Indicators News (SINET). A quarterly newsletter studying indicators of social change (http://www.soc.duke.edu/dept/sinet/pub_info.html).

The Utne Reader. A bimonthly magazine of original articles on values and social change as well as compilations of relevant articles from other publications (http://www.utne.com).

Technology and Science

CNET. A daily online newsletter about computer technology and the Internet. Subscriptions are free (http://www.news.com/index.html).

Information Week (http://www.informationweek.com)

PC Magazine (http://www.zdnet.com/pcmag)

Technotrends Newsletter (http://www.burrus.com/monthlypublication.html)

Appendix B
Glossary

Active Learning
Conceives of learning as a form of active mental work that involves the internal mental construction of new ideas and associations, instead of just the passive reception of facts.

Baby Boom Generation
Born between 1943 and 1960, this generation grew up during a time of historically unprecedented prosperity, indulged by their parents, and free from the financial fears and other major threats that characterized their parents' lives.

Community of Practice
An informal network of people engaged in a particular profession, occupation, or job function who actively seek to work more effectively and to understand their work more fully.

Distributed Learning
Allowing learners to learn wherever they want, whenever they want, at any point during their lifespan, with the assistance of modern communications technologies.

Generation X
Born between 1961 and 1981, this generation grew up in the full swing of U.S. consumer culture and watched their parents work long hours to pay off homes in the suburbs. Since the world didn't present to X-ers what they initially expected, when given the chance, they can be reluctant to commit. Skepticism is often their defense mechanism.

Generational Synergy
When the different generations within an organization appreciate each other's virtues, support each other, and work together in creative interaction.

Global Metaculture
The emerging international culture that fuses entertainment, news, commerce, and language into a synthetic global culture.

Globalization
Increasing levels of interdependence over vast distances across a wide variety of spheres, including economic, political, cultural, environmental, etc.

Glocalization

An emerging concept describing the growing synergy between globalization and localization that is creating an interdependent world.

Group Forming Networks

A form of network structure that allows each node to directly communicate with any other, creating nearly infinite possibilities for the formation of sub-groups.

Inclusivity

An approach to differences in cultural and personal perspectives that emphasizes understanding and preserving valuable differences and using them as a resource for creativity and problem solving.

Infoglut

The deluge of information pouring into our lives, making it increasingly difficult to find valuable, meaningful knowledge in all the data and information that flows in our direction.

Larger Purpose

The contributions you make to society through your major activities.

Learning Culture

A learner centered education environment facilitating collaborative learning processes that can be pursued at any time, from any location.

Living Organizations

Organizations that rely on self-organizing structures, purpose and values, trust, and knowledge sharing to adapt and evolve to meet emerging opportunities.

Localization

Conscious strategies to provide local communities and organizations greater control over their own political and economic futures.

Mass customization

The ability to produce large quantities of products while customizing them to the unique characteristics of local or niche markets.

Meaning

The "why" that gives significance to all the "whats" and "hows" and helps us make sense of our lives and organizations.

Millennial Generation

Born between 1982 and the present, this generation has grown up in an era of unprecedented prosperity, and tend to be optimistic, earnest, and team oriented. They have grown up leading the most structured and supervised lives of any generation in living memory.

Multi-Local

The ability of local associations to *directly* communicate and collaborate with other local associations—without the assistance of a national organization.

NGO

Nongovernmental organizations, typically nonprofit institutions of a civil nature working in objectively various fields of development, such as scientific, charitable, educational, legal religious, or other fields.

Positive Deviance

Identifying unusually good practices that stand out from the norm and trying to integrate them into the standard practices of an organization.

Purpose

The ends that we work together to achieve.

Transnational Civil Society

The hundreds of nongovernmental organizations (NGOs) that monitor the behavior of corporations, governments, and other organizations, and curb abuses by bringing them to public attention.

Transparency

Operating in an open and accountable manner, and providing the public information it can use to evaluate an organization's performance.

Self-Organizing Structures

The spontaneous order that can emerge from many networked agents freely choosing how to respond to multiple options.

Silent Generation

Born between 1925 and 1942, this generation emerged from WWII with a "can do" attitude and sense of confidence that made them leaders and institution-builders.

Strategic Communication

Discussions that inform boards, volunteers, and staff about how to incorporate new insights on key issues into the organization's culture. The creation of new knowledge around issues and future trends likely to affect the organization will emerge to foster the development of key future strategies.

Appendix C
The ASAE Foundation Futures Scan
Online Scanning Process

The seven strategic issues described in this report emerged from a ten-month, Internet-based futures scan computer conference that involved over one hundred creative thinkers in the association community and a score of futurists and guest experts. At the beginning of the process, five broad themes were adopted as an initial framework for discussion:

1. **Converging Technologies, New Economies.** Revolutions in computers and communications, materials and manufacturing, and many other areas are coming together and strengthening each other. The resulting acceleration of technological change will transform the infrastructures and economies of every society. Efficient new organizational forms built around networked computing and the Internet will force existing organizations to renew themselves or become obsolete.

2. **Demographic Destinies, Human Choices.** Between now and 2020, nearly as much population growth will occur as occurred from the beginning of human history to World War I—almost all of it in developing nations. Those whom we call minorities today will constitute over a third of the population by 2020 and will be a majority by later in the century. The aging 70-million-strong Baby Boomers will continue to dominate the work force, but after 2005, the Millennial generation—the Boomers' children—will enter the work force in large numbers.

3. **Global Societies, Local Communities.** Events are marching simultaneously in opposite directions, toward both globalization and localization. Globalization will accelerate exponentially as low-cost phone, fax, and paging; high-speed Internet access; teleconferencing; and automatic language translation become available everywhere. Localization is appearing in many forms. Nearly all advanced nations are shifting more decision-making authority to states or provinces. The Internet is spawning new, nongeographic communities of interest.

4. **Learning Organizations, Visionary Leaders.** Constant learning is the key to organizational responsiveness—responsiveness to trends and emerging issues in the external environment and responsiveness to members, buyers of an organization's products and services, employees, and partners. Learning organiza-

tions require flatter, more networked, structures to facilitate organizationwide knowledge sharing and more decentralized decision making to respond quickly to market conditions. Learning organizations require visionary leaders who can clarify aspirations and inspire others to pursue them rather than merely reacting to immediate circumstances.

5. **Noble Aspirations, Lasting Legacies.** Modern writers have called attention to the Greek concept of *paideia* as the highest aspiration yet developed for human progress. Paideia was conceived as the central cultural project, the task of making life itself an art form, with the person the work of art. The collective goal was to design Athenian society, and all its institutions, to bring all its members to the fullest development of their highest powers. We cannot emulate ancient Greece, but we can explore how our own institutions might evolve to support not just economic growth but human growth.

Each theme was designed to be discussed in two months and featured guest experts who were invited to engage in week-long Chautauqua discussions with participants. At the end of each theme, a synthesis and review of the major topics discussed was posted to the online forum for review and discussion about what topics and ideas are most important for the association community of discussions. The association participants in the online forum could give their feedback on which topics would be most important to the association community. The list below is a sample of the large variety of topics that emerged in the online dialogue:

- Attracting the Millennial Generation
- Work and Family in the 21st Century
- Aging of Boomers
- Dealing with New Diversity
- Mobilizing Cultural Creatives
- Downshifting—Integration of Work and Life
- Values, Ethics, and Spirituality
- Advancing America and the World
- What Associations Can Do to Genuinely Support Learning
- Social Capital: Increasing or Decreasing
- Global Problems, Global Solutions
- Letting Go of Stereotypes

- Leaving a Legacy
- Future of Work
- What Is Glocalization?
- Radical Transparency
- Protests Against Globalization
- Going Local
- Learning Organizations
- Digital Governance
- Dealing with Constant Technological Change
- Virtual Associations
- Distributed Learning
- Attention Economy
- Good Tech: Associations Influencing Technological Change

The follow are excerpts from the community of practice online discussion.

Topic: Work and Family in the 21st Century

Fusion Family

There is general agreement that the pace of life is accelerating and that free time is becoming one of the most precious commodities for working adults. This acceleration, which some pundits have dubbed "The Great Blur" is a key force that is driving lifestyle changes in the American family. Family lifestyles are increasingly being defined by the way in which families approach this critical issue. What is emerging is a range of family lifestyles bounded by two extreme approaches: Outsourcing and Downshifting.

Outsourcing

Outsourcing in family life uses money—often from two-career couples—to purchase essential but time-consuming family services. Day care and home childcare is the primary family function that is commonly outsourced, with cleaning and laundry services to a somewhat lesser extent. However, in recent years, the scope of family activities that are being subcontract has expanded considerably. Personal assistants will come to your house and precook meals for your family. Services will plan you child's birthday party, or assemble family albums from a box of random pictures. As these services become more common and inexpensive, the line between "family" and "family services" will grow less distinct.

Downshifting

Downshifting involves limiting the material consumption of the family in order to gain more time to pursue wider personal interests or a more extensive family life. Whether it is a desire to "quit the rat-race," live a more holistic and sustainable lifestyle, or allow a parent to stay at home with a child full-time, downshifters are willing to trade material wealth for a better quality of life. Families are beginning to move beyond the suburbs to rural small towns to enjoy the peaceful and unhurried lifestyle of the country. A movement toward Voluntary Simplicity provides advice and justifications for stepping off the treadmill of the corporate career path. Increasing numbers of children are being home-schooled by full-time parents, who are willing to forego a free public school education for their children. The rising popularity of telecommuting, temping, and independent consulting will enable increasing numbers of dissatisfied workers to choose a new balance among work, play, and home.

- What new associations will need to be created in order to support the new family services that are being outsourced?
- How will associations play a role in the quality-of-life explorations of downshifters?
- What impacts will new family structures have on associations?

Excerpts from Community of Practice Discussions

"I think many of us outsource not because we have no choice (not enough time), but because we want to spend our time in better ways. We would rather be at a daughter's soccer game—or even working longer hours to get ahead—than cleaning the house or preparing a meal. In other words, the downshifters and the outsourcers have the same objective: more quality time. They just choose different approaches."
Tom Conger

"How many of us ignore the value and benefit of creating flexible work arrangements unless some life altering major event creates the need to accommodate employee's desires?" **Mark J. Golden, CAE**

"I haven't reached a downshifting phase but I certainly have made some choices among what I can realistically accomplish in a day/week and still enjoy my life. My experience indicates that we have to make some choices and adaptations to allow quality time with our families. I do want to pose a question—doesn't every generation struggle with balancing their time? Is it a natural part of 'growing up' when we feel rushed and pulled in many directions?" **Sherry Keramidas, Ph.D., CAE**

"My association has numerous chapters, and the executive directors of most of these chapters are struggling with getting members to attend meetings or education events. However, their golf outings, Bar-B-Q's, and other social-type events are sold out. As most participants agreed in our previous discussion group, there are few places other than an association where people can get together and have fun with peers and discuss similar professional interests on the side. Is the popularity of social-type events because stressed-out, busy people will take time out for them when they won't take time out to sit in a seminar? Then, what would the applications be? Do we (1) meet the needs of stressed out people or (2) can we do more within our organizations to help bring more balance to members' lives, educate them, do good works, etc.? Could be we have to provide more of #1 in order to generate the revenue to provide #2." **Frances Shuping, CAE**

"An interesting point has been raised about seeing the association as part of the fusion family. I would think many individuals do see their association colleagues as a crtical part of their personal fusion family and turn to them as an ongoing means of support and friendship. Playing with that notion a bit might cause us to think about service delivery and program content, etc. It brings up that notion of 'safe space' that we talked about in the previous module." **Jeffrey Cufaude**

Topic: Experience Economy

In recent history, as goods become commoditized, companies differentiated those goods on the basis of value-added services—and the service economy emerged. Now, services are becoming commoditized, and if Joseph Pine and James Gilmore, authors of *The Experience Economy*, are right, organizations will differentiate their services by experiences. They will use services as the stage and goods as props to move to the next layer in economic value. In other words, in the same way goods were once superseded by services, services will be superceded by experiences.

The authors encourage others to follow the lead of companies like Disney and AOL and stage rich, compelling experiences for their customers/clients/members. Organizations in the experience business will orchestrate memorable events, charging for the time spent in the experience according to the value of the transformation that the experience offers.

To design a memorable and personally engaging experience, Pine and Gilmore suggest creating a consistent theme throughout the experience—layered with positive cues that reinforce the theme and removing negative cues that distract from or contradict the theme. They also suggest engaging all five senses and offering memorabilia that commemorates the experience.

- How would conferences and conventions change in the experience economy?
- Studies have already shown that, globally, some population groups are developing post-material values. What does this mean for associations?
- How might compensation and rewards change in the experience economy?

Excerpts from Community of Practice Discussions

"This dialogue reminds me of a story I read in the *Wall Street Journal* the other day. Theaters in New York City are trying to enhance the show experience by having the audience get involved at the end of the show. The hope is that this will have the audience leaving happy and remember the show favorably.

"The show Saturday Night Fever has everyone get up to dance at the end—whether they want to or not. Remarks from the audience to the reporter was that it was a forced experience that did not hide the weakness in the show.

"Point being, experiences need to build on quality and enhance value. By themselves, they mean nothing." **Janet B. Bray, CAE**

"Most have talked about the experience economy in relatively negative terms, but when looked at in the above way, it's a powerful way of thinking that some very important core values and needs may be the new drivers of what is important in the larger global environment. If more and more people are motivated by higher needs (*e.g.*, emotional, psychological, relational, and spiritual), then we can't help but live in a better, healthier world. I do think that such an evolution would have significant impacts for association." **Mark Anderson, CAE**

Topic: Attention Economy

On the Internet, through much of its past, the bulk of its present and the foreseeable future, prices often don't matter at all. People don't seem to want to pay—or charge—for the most popular goods and services on the Internet. Newspapers and magazines are putting their content on the Web for everyone to read—for free. Enthusiasts will spend hours designing, writing, and managing their own Web sites without any expectation of compensation for all their effort. While this may seem somewhat illogical from a conventional economic perspective, a new model of economic thinking is beginning to explain these behaviors as examples of an emerging Attention Economy.

The new attention economy has certain important characteristics:

- Attention is a scarce human resource
- Attention is the critical companion to information. Having vast quantities of information available is of little value unless the intended audience pays attention to it.
- In its pure form, the attention economy does not involve exchanges of money or other conventional economic activity.
- Mechanisms of property defense and control (secrecy, privacy) tend to diminish the generation of attention, while openness tends to attract attention.

Attention is playing an increasingly important role in the new economy, but the secondary effects of attention economics need a fuller exploration. Does the need to draw attention place too much emphasis on glitz and packaging instead of the quality of the content? Does the attention economics elevate the status of celebrities (who are contemporary attention magnets) to an even higher level? Alternatively, could this emphasis on nonfinancial compensation form the foundation of a new sustainable economics that focuses more on gaining attention than consuming material goods?

- What would it mean to associations for board members or executives to be selected for their attention-attracting abilities, instead of conventional business skills?
- What new activities could associations engage in to attract attention?
- What tactics might associations have to resort to generate attention?

Excerpts from Community of Practice Discussions

"The real problem is how to keep attention once it has been grabbed. It's the content. That content may be information or knowledge. It may be a sympathetic and understanding listener. It may be a sense of community with others of a similar interest or background. It may be a sense of shared purpose. It may be a perceived net financial benefit. In any event, competition for associations will increase." **Henry Ernstthal, JD, CAE**

Topic: Social Capital: Increasing or Decreasing

Bowling Alone by Robert Putnam has been mentioned several times in different discussions. The title of this book refers to Putnam's famous discovery that although just as many Americans go bowling today as they did 30 years ago, far fewer of them belong to bowling leagues and clubs. So they "bowl alone," a haunting metaphor for the alienation and atomization that Putnam believes infects contemporary America. Putnam's discovery has been expanded into a full-fledged book documenting the decline of "social capital" in American life.

One the other hand, there is *The Ladd Report*. This relatively recent book by Everett Ladd documents the increase of social capital in American society. Ladd was the president of the Roper Center for Public Opinion Research, and he musters an impressive array of evidence supporting his thesis.

According to *The Ladd Report*: "Voluntarism and other facets of civic engagement are shaped by three separate sets of factors: (1) core moral commitments, such as understandings of individual responsibility; (2) stages of socioeconomic development, which determine relevant resources; and (3) short-term forces that variously encourage or dispirit the population."

Whether Putnam or Ladd is ultimately correct is something the social science scholars will definitively establish…about a generation from now. In the meantime, it will be interesting to hear from those on both sides of the social capital question what the growth or the decline in social capital means for associations.

If social capital is declining, do associations become less important, or do they become more important as "bigger fish in a smaller pond?"

If social capital is on the increase, does increased networking among the grass roots pose a threat to associations, or does this only increase the opportunities for expanding membership and relevance?

Excerpts from Community of Practice Discussions

"For the purposes of discussion, I'll just borrow Putnam's definition:

"Just as a screwdriver (physical capital) or a college education (human capital) can increase productivity (both individual and collective), so too social contacts affect the productivity of individuals and groups.

"Whereas physical capital refers to physical objects and human capital refers to properties of individuals, social capital refers to connections among individuals—social networks and the norms of reciprocity and trustworthiness that arise from them." **Mark Justman**

"I guess my first impression of this discussion is that basically social capital changes over time and develops new patterns that are impacted by society. The old picnics in the neighborhood still take place, but they may be the block parties in cities, or parties in your apartment lobbies. I also think that different cultures have their own way of doing them. Like the *casitas* in the Cuban culture. Sometimes we do not realize that volunteering takes place in all cultures and throughout society but it could be helping a neighbor, not joining an association. If an organization makes it easy for me to volunteer, I will make the time." **Joan Carolyn Kupyer, CAE**

"Associations must learn this rule: 'If you can't get people to take the jobs you've got, change the job.'" **Henry L. Ernstthal, CAE**

While many of the topics received some discussion, a limited number were judged to be (1) highly relevant for the future of associations, (2) relatively new insights deserving of wider attention, and (3) developed enough in the conversation, or in the literature, to be able to describe them well. Topics that met these basic criteria were selected and refined for the next stage of the process: focus group testing.

Focus groups played a key role in reframing the topics to make them more directly relevant to the association community at large. Topic digests were distributed to focus group participants at major conferences and special focus groups convened at ASAE. Responses were collected and integrated into the final formulations of the seven issues. The focus groups received a broad range of commentary from the association community at a relatively early stage.

As a representative example, the Generational Synergy chapter began the focus group process as a chapter that focused only on the Millennial Generation. Many focus group participants felt that it was the entire pattern of generational interaction that was more relevant, so the final version of the chapter was reformulated to take a broader approach to generational issues.

After all the focus group testing was conducted, the topics were reshaped and combined into the final seven ideas presented in this report. The final form—and content—has been deeply influenced by this collaborative and interactive process. At every stage of development, group feedback has shaped the next iteration of the material leading to a report that has been shaped by the many perspectives expressed by various experts, participants, and commentators. The final report integrates many threads of conversation into seven coherent concepts that association leaders can use to explore and shape the future.

Appendix D
Guidelines for Online Futures Scanning

1. **Threaded discussion for long-term conversation, linear for short-term.** Online discussion software generally has two different messages formats: linear and threaded. In the linear format, there can be up to dozens of topics, and for each topic, comments are added to the document at the end of the page. The threaded format has a similar topic structure, but handles replies differently. Replies in the threaded format can be directed to specific messages, giving rise to a variety of threaded subtopics. The threaded system is better for long-term, multi-topic discussions; however, the intensity of a linear format is effective for focused conversations with guest participants.

2. **Introduce topics gradually.** Resist the temptation to start out the process by putting online as much content as possible to maximize interest. Front-loading the discussion runs the risk of quickly burning out the participants. Instead of providing value, you may overwhelming your participants. Focus on pacing the introduction of new material and topics to keep the conversational manageable. This can help to revitalize conversations as old topics become exhausted.

3. **Interspersed face-to-face meetings can help bond the online community of practice.** This can range from a single, initial instructional meeting to brief participants on the process, to occasional intermittent meetings that happen to be convenient, to regular meetings where that is possible. An initial meeting is recommended. Any face-to-face meeting between online discussion participants will help to deepen their enthusiasm. It gives participants a chance to put faces to the names they've seen virtually and reinforces the fact that there are real people who are paying attention to the comments that get typed up onto a solitary computer screen.

4. **Recognize that even online, there are extraverts and introverts.** Online discussion forums can give shy public speakers a forum to fully express themselves, but other people find it more comfortable to generally observe and comment occasionally. The mix of active participants and observational participants is perfectly normal. Recruit members from a broad cross-section of your membership.

5. **Guest participants and "speakers" can effectively focus the discussion.** Get respected thought leaders involved from the start. This will build energy and excitement around the topic. The ASAE Foundation invited guest experts to field questions and lead discussion for a week at time. Many were willing to share their time and insights with the community for longer periods. The combination of a limited-time commitment, and the ability to respond at their leisure, made it doable for experts with a hectic schedule. Time pressures also made participants pay closer attention and try to get their questions answered and make their points during the limited time the expert was scheduled to be online.

6. **Promote the discussion to participants though e-mail updates.** Some participants get distracted by other concerns and may get out of the habit of keeping abreast of the online discussion. Periodic e-mails to all participants' can reignite their interest and get them back into the flow of the discussion. These e-mail updates can consist of announcements of new guest participants coming online, provocative quotes from participants, or announcements of new conversation topics.

7. **Periodic summarization can help participants stay on track.** The spontaneous qualities of online discussions can cause conversations to evolve into entirely unexpected directions. This is a valuable aspect of online discussions, but it can become difficult to track the evolution of conversations as they move beyond the confines of their topic labels. It can be helpful to briefly summarize the course of preceding conversation—both to help part-time participants get up to speed and to help regulars get a better perspective on what has—and has not—been discussed during the process. Participant reactions to summaries can be a critical way to distill insights and interests of members into a manageable document that all participants can read.

Appendix E
The Importance of Environmental Scanning

Many organizations…are remarkably out of touch with the wider world. Their executives may be so preoccupied with near-field problems and issues that they feel they have no time to think about the far field. These organizations tend to be the sitting ducks that take the worst punishment when the shock wave hits.

—Karl Albrecht,
*The Northbound Train,*1994

Recognizing that current information about emerging issues is essential for discovering tomorrow's opportunities, boards and staff are devoting more time to research and environmental scanning. *What is environmental scanning?* It is simply a systematic and continuous effort to search for important cues about how the world is changing and how they will affect your organization. Although there is no one right way or approach, environmental scanning generally has the following characteristics:

- A broad range of issues are examined, including economic, global, political, technological, and social trends;

- Information is gathered from a variety of sources, such as literature reviews, surveys, interviews with experts, focus groups, scan panels, site visits, etc.;

- Leading-edge thinkers are sought out both inside and outside the industry or profession being scanned; and

- "Outside of the box" thinking is encouraged by studying trends and changes occurring in unrelated industries or professions.

The advantages of environmental scanning are compelling. It enables the association to be more nimble and avoid the costly mistake of reacting too slowly to foreseeable events. It is also an essential tool to uncover ways to implement and manage change successfully.

It is important to recognize that a plug-and-play formula for scanning does not exist—there are almost as many ways to scan as there are associations!

Association executives should be aware that creating a comprehensive, ongoing scanning program is a task measured in years, not months or weeks. There are two reasons for this:

1. It takes time and exploration to determine the mix of information sources best suited for your association's unique situation. You should expect to spend the first six months to a year exploring a wide variety of publications, Web sites, and information-retrieval services.

2. Engaging your board, staff, and volunteers in the process won't happen overnight. You will need to experiment with different types of scanning assignments and figure out which people are best suited for a particular scanning assignment.

The Routine Three Sources of Scanning Information

If you are like most association executives, your scanning horizon is limited to three major sources:

Add Diversity to Your Scanning
by Seeking Other Sources and Perspectives

Association executives need to broaden the range of their scanning activities:

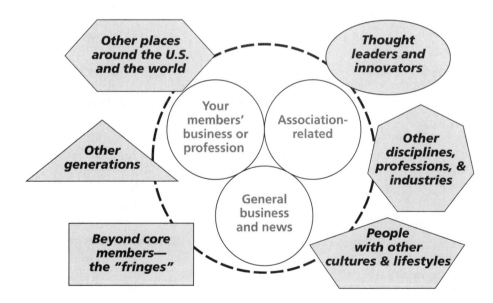

Listen to all segments within your membership

Are you hearing from all possible facets of your membership? Here are different segments that can offer perspectives about your changing environment:

- Generations—Silents, Boomers, Gen X-ers, and Millennials
- Ethnicity
- Gender
- Geographic location:
  - rural and urban
  - different regions of the United States
  - international
- Special interest areas or special interest groups
- Types/size of business
- Technology sophistication level
- Career phase
- Income
- Allegiance categories
- Education (level and types of degrees)
- Segments based on purchase behaviors
- Volunteers and nonvolunteers
- Level of satisfaction with membership
- Years of membership
- Segments based on rate of growth (*e.g.,* fastest growing segments of your membership and/or slowest growing or declining segment)
- Special Physical Characteristics
- Other: _____

Ex-members, nonmembers, and potential members

This is a critical category that must not be overlooked in your scanning efforts. Every association, if it truly seeks to understand its environment, must talk to those outside its membership base.

Seek out those members with distinctly different perspectives

- Thought-leaders and innovators. Which people within your membership are recognized as being on the leading edge (*e.g.,* pioneering new ways of doing business, innovative use of technology, conducting bold new research, etc.)?
- The futurists and scanners in your midst. Are there members who do scanning and future thinking for their companies or organizations?
- "Fringe" groups within your membership. These are the folks who stand out from your core membership—often they are the gadflies who do things differently (*e.g.,* run socially responsible businesses, have different lifestyles, etc.).
- Those members who have just entered the profession or business, including recent college graduates, or seasoned professionals making a career transition.
- Those members who are among the first wave to be affected by an emerging trend (*e.g.,* consolidations, facing global competition, etc.).
- Diverse members who have different perspectives and life experiences.

The hidden expertise among your board, staff, and volunteers

Are you seeking out the "hidden" expertise resident among your board, staff, and volunteers? Many of them have valuable career experiences, education, or hobbies that give them expertise in the topic areas you wish to scan. Be sure to take an inventory of these skills and interest areas.

Those Who Have Regular Contact with Your Association

Every association has a wealth of contacts via the vendors and organizations with which it normally does business. Take the following inventory:

People and Organizations with Whom Your Association Has Regular Contact

- Vendors
- Exhibitors
- Hotels and Resorts
- Affinity Partners
- Related Associations
- Consultants
- Speakers and Education Providers

How Might They Contribute to Your Association's Scanning Activities?

What is their area of expertise? (*e.g.*, technology, human resources, etc.)

Does their company/organization conduct environmental scanning on a regular basis? If so:

- What kinds of information are they collecting?
- What might they share with your organization?
- Who in their organization would be willing to participate in one of your association's scanning activities?
- What sources of information and people do these organizations use in their scanning efforts?

Among this list of contacts, who are the smartest and most innovative thinkers? How can you involve them in your scanning activities?

Beyond the Boundaries of Your Association— Seeking Outside Perspectives

To truly broaden the scope of your scanning activities, you need to talk regularly to people who are in fields totally unrelated to those of your association.

To add breadth to your scanning activities, include the following types of people:

- Thought leaders in business, government, technology, and social issues. (Or seek out people who work inside innovative companies and organizations.)

- Different generations—especially young people (*e.g.,* grade school on up to college students).

- Across disciplines, professions, or industries. Look outside the association profession and the business/profession served by your members.

- Futurists.

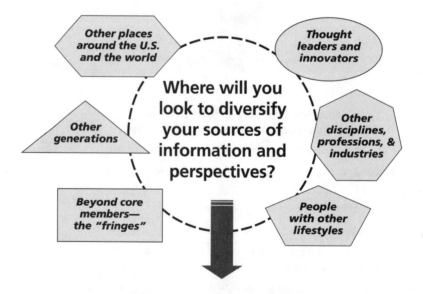

Diversification of Perspectives and Sources Worksheet

Seek a Diversity of Perspectives and Sources

List New Sources and People To Use in Your Scanning Efforts

_____

_____

_____

_____

Instructions for Reporting on a Trend or Issue

When reporting on a trend or issue, follow this format:

Person Reporting: _____

Trend or Issue: _____

Information Sources Used

List people, Web sites (include URLs), publications, etc., used to gather the information for this report.	Rate the quality of each source (Excellent, good, fair, poor)

Summary of Findings

Provide an objective overview of your findings. Provide a brief background and facts associated with the trend or issue.

Key Insights

Based on what you have learned, address the following:

Implications/Consequences—What are the most important implications or consequences for the association? In particular, point out opportunities or threats.

Action Required

"Urgency Factor"—What is the time frame? Is immediate action or attention required?

Appendix F
Trends Affecting Associations

A brief overview of the 14 trends discussed in *Facing the Future: A Report on the Major Trends and Issues Facing Associations*

Leadership's Role
Adopting a new set of leadership characteristics for association boards and staff will be necessary to move into the twenty-first century.

Value/Return on Investment (ROI)
Meeting rising member expectations and a greater demand for a return on dues investment will drive association redesign.

Responsiveness
Keeping up with external changes and responding rapidly to members' emerging needs will require associations to become "fast, fluid, and flexible."

Governance
Replacing current governance models that are too slow and cumbersome to deal with an increasingly complex, fast-paced environment will require a cultural shift for most associations.

Revenue Sources
The need for new revenue sources will drive associations to become more innovative in seeking out new partners and nontraditional sources of income.

Technology Usage
The profound and beneficial impact of technology usage will be felt through its increasing capability to link people, build relationships, and foster communities.

Change Loops
Mastering the unplanned changes and unexpected consequences (*i.e.,* "change loops") that do not fall neatly inside the time frame of the traditional planning calendar or scheduled board meetings will require a new mind-set about budgeting and other planning processes.

Generational Issues

The generational shifts among staff, board, and members will fundamentally alter the culture of associations due to shifts in member perception of and loyalty to the association, differing preferences for programs and services, and degree of volunteer involvement.

Workforce

Securing a qualified workforce with the proper mix of business, technical, and social skills combined with diverse life experiences will demand greater skill, time, and effort from the association executive.

Outsourcing and Co-Sourcing

Gaining maximum advantage from outsourcing or co-sourcing will require associations to carefully distinguish core from noncore functions and to identify strategic as well as cost-saving benefits.

Competition and Alliances

Increasing vulnerability to competition will require associations to become more vigilant about new types of competitors and to seek out nontraditional allies.

Consolidations and Mergers

As consolidations and mergers occur with greater speed and unpredictability, associations will have to become more proactive in dealing with the resulting impact on revenues, services, and membership categories.

Globalization

As their members become less and less bounded by geography, time zones, culture, or language in their business and professional relationships, associations will have to redefine their boundaries accordingly.

Image Building

Increasing public scrutiny and competition will lead associations (professional and philanthropic organizations as well as trades) to defend their members' credibility and promote the unique value of their services or activities.

Appendix G

Exercise 1
Provocative Questions Lead to Provocative Futures

Over the course of the ASAE Foundation's Futures Scan, association executives raised many provocative questions about the relevance of associations and the very assumptions on which they were built. The following list is a representation of those questions from the online discussion forum and focus groups. We can use them to challenge and provoke our assumptions:

1. In what ways will associations (and the members of associations) change the manner in which they measure the value of "belonging?"

2. Based upon all the social, economic and communicative evolution that is occurring, how do associations evolve to new organizational models that will allow them to shed the restraints of governance, money, etc., and serve members in a quicker, more responsive nature that is being expected by people in this "Internet" world?

3. What do associations need to do to genuinely support learning?

4. How is technology shaping the culture and community of associations?

5. How do we get leadership to "see the light" and change to be more inclusive?

6. What are the environmental factors that have permitted and encouraged the growth and vitality of associations, and how stable are they?

7. How can associations offer more meaning to younger employees?

8. How can multi-generational work teams be maximized?

9. How do we create the "Three Generation Association" and perhaps later the "Four Generation Association" that appeals to people across generational lines?

10. How can associations adapt to and even promote a more cyclical life pattern that allows periods of heavy involvement, lighter involvement, retraining?

11. How can we plan to take advantage of the coming retirement boom by expanding the use of volunteers?

12. How can we create more flexible staffing patterns that allow individuals of all ages to stop in/stop out for varied work patterns that meet their personal reinvention needs at a particular point in their life?

13. What role can distance learning play to help close the knowing and doing gap or can it?

14. How do you address diversity in an online venue?

15. What do you think is the responsibility of associations to acquaint their members with Internet tools?

16. How is informal learning in the organization captured, shared, and leveraged on an ongoing basis?

17. What are the personal competencies or aspects of organizational culture that are crucial for a learning organization?

18. How global will associations need to become?

19. How can associations create meaningful community in a world that is scaling up and fragmenting at the same time?

20. How will association advocacy need to change as more public policy decisions are made at the state and local level?

21. Is an organization whose members are cosmetically diverse but who all think alike truly diverse?

22. How can we make the bridge to this future for our members and leaders? Or do we have to wait for the Gen-Xers or the Millennials?

Exercise 1A
Using Provocative Questions To Create Provocative Futures

Objective: To create future scenarios that are deliberately thought-provoking. Participants respond to provocative questions and use their answers to challenge old assumptions to discover important ways the future may be very different from today.

Time: 60-75 minutes

Format: Small groups of 4-8 each

Materials: Flip chart, markers, masking tape, and handouts of these instructions and "Provocative Questions Lead to Provocative Futures" sheet

Instructions

5 mins.
- Review the objective for the exercise with the group.
- Divide into small groups of 4-8.
- Small groups select a recorder.
- Distribute copies of these instructions and the "Provocative Questions Lead to Provocative Futures" sheet.

10 mins.
- Review the following instructions for group discussions and report-backs:
  - Read the "Provocative Questions Lead to Provocative Futures" sheet.

  Optional:
  - Brainstorm three *additional* provocative questions relevant to their association's future.
  - Record the questions on a flip chart sheet and post it for clear viewing.
  - Choose *three* questions to explore during the rest of the exercise.

TIP: *Any three questions can be chosen from the handout sheet and/or the flip chart sheets created by the small groups.*

- Discuss what implications the questions have for the future.

- Summarize the discussion by creating a "why this is critical to our association's future" statement for *each* of the three questions.

- Deliberately choose a "provocative" answer to each question.

TIP: *Deliberately choose answers that will take the association outside its normal "comfort zone."*

15-30 mins.   Report Out

Reporter for each group describes the future it envisioned:

- The three questions the group chose and the related "why" statements.

- At least three ways their future will be different.

- What they are looking forward to.

- What they are dreading.

20-30 mins.   Discuss together:

- What elements are similar in all the futures presented?

- How do the futures differ? Is there any significance in the differences?

- What other provocative questions concerning the future come to mind?

- What important issues or trends have we identified that need to be closely monitored or researched?

Exercise 2

Why Is It?

In a world where members are demanding greater value and return on investment for their dues dollars, it is important to uncover the areas where your members are not being served. These represent the danger zones where new competition can emerge.

Examining "Why is it?" questions will help you discover these critical service areas. Consider:

- Maxwell House would have been better prepared strategically if it had been savvy enough to ask, "Why is it that a great cup of coffee is available for $1 at Starbucks but not from the airport concessions that sell the decades-old Maxwell House brand from General Foods?"*

- IBM, a few years back, could have avoided its downturn if it had asked, "Why is it you can get patient assistance from a Home Depot clerk when selecting a $2.70 package of screws, but you can't get any advice when purchasing a $2,700 personal computer from IBM's direct ordering service?"*

- Lotus could have protected its dominant position in the spreadsheet market by asking, "Why is it that you can buy intuitive, engaging, and intelligent software for a Sega video game, but after a decade on the market, Lotus 1-2-3 had basically the same look, feel, and function?"*

* Quotations are from *The Discipline of Market Leaders: Choose Your Customers, Narrow Your Focus, Dominate Your Market* by Michael Treacy and Fred Wiersema. (New York: Addison-Wesley Publishing Company, 1995).

Now imagine what kinds of "Why is it?" questions your members might be asking. It is especially important to consider what questions your members will be asking *two or three years from now.* For example, in a few years your members could be asking:

- Why is it I get the daily news and industry information down loaded in a customized format via the Web, but I can't get _____ from my association?

- Why is it that kids in college have access to the latest and most exciting ways to receive education, but I can't get _____ when I attend the annual meeting?

- Why is it I can buy auto insurance anytime of the day or night, but I can't get _____ from my association after 5 p.m.?

- Why is it _____, but _____?

- Why is it _____, but _____?

Exercise 2A
Why Is It?

Objectives: This exercise helps participants to:

- View the association from the average members' point of view.

- Develop a set of questions that improves anticipation of members' evolving needs.

Time: 1.5-2 hours

Format: Small groups of 4-8 each

Materials: Flip chart, markers, masking tape, self-adhesive dots
Handouts of these instructions and the "Why Is It?" worksheet

Instructions

5 mins.
- Review the objectives for the exercise with the group.

- Divide into small groups of 4-8.

- Small groups select a recorder and a reporter.

- Distribute instructions and the "Why Is It?" worksheet to each participant.

- Tell participants to read the "Why Is It?" worksheet.

10-15 mins.
- Review the following instructions for the *first* small group discussion and report-backs.

- Ask participants if they have any questions about what to do.

- Small groups:

    - Use the worksheet to generate at least *five* "Why is it?" questions.

TIP: *The group doesn't have to restrict itself to the suggested questions on the worksheet.*

    - Record the questions on flip chart sheet(s).

TIP: *All ideas must be in the form of a question.*

10 mins. • The reporter from each group posts its list of questions and responds to comments or questions about the list from participants.

15-20 mins. • Post all the lists.

• Ask the entire group to identify the top three or four "Why Is It?" questions from among all the questions listed.

• Combine and consolidate questions as necessary.

• Consider any new questions that emerge during the discussion.

• Write the top three or four questions on the flip chart and post for clear viewing.

15-20 mins. • Review the following instructions for the second round of small group discussions and report-backs.

• Ask participants if they have any questions about what to do.

• Small groups:

  • Use the top three or four questions to brainstorm the "Top 10 Ways" your association can be more responsive to members and deliver greater value to them.

  • Make sure there are a minimum of two examples in each of the following categories:

    – Totally new programs, services, or ventures the association should pursue.

    – Major enhancements or overhauls of existing programs or services.

    – Programs, products, or services that should be retired.

15-20 mins. • Reporters from small groups take turns reporting a way to deliver value.

• Compile a master list on the flip chart.

• Continue to add new ideas to the master list until each group's "top 10" ideas have been reported.

15 mins.

- Give each participant 10 self-adhesive dots.

- Ask participants to select the top 10 ways to deliver value to members by putting a dot next to each of their choices.

- Tally up the choices and record participants' "Top Ten Ways to Deliver Value."

- Discuss participants' choices.

Exercise 3
Storytelling

Your subgroup will create a "mini-story" about the future of your association. It should reflect a time period of three to five years from now. Later on, someone from your group will be responsible for telling the story to the entire group. The story should take no more than a minute to tell.

As you create the story, keep in mind the following:

- Use the issues your subgroup chose as most critical.

- Begin the process by creating a provocative headline that describes something about your association's future in two to five years. Be creative and imaginative in thinking about how the issues might play out in the future. Choose a *memorable headline* to describe that future (*e.g.,* "The Age of Unreason," "Happy Days Are Here Again," etc.).

- The story can demonstrate how these issues are interrelated.

- Place the story's time frame at least two years from now, but no more than five years from today.

- Remember, the future you are describing should be significantly different than today (*i.e.,* there is something surprising, unexpected, unanticipated about it).

- Base the story on facts and implications from changes you know are occurring. The story should be plausible as well as surprising.

Work quickly and intuitively. Rely on your "hunches" about the future. Do not get bogged down trying to explain or defend your choices.

Exercise 3A

Storytelling
A Powerful Technique To Analyze Change in your Environment

Objective: This exercise will help the group organize information and deal with its complexity. The group can use storytelling to analyze its changing environment, envision the future, and develop strategic and business plans.

Time: 3 hours

Format: This technique works best with a minimum of 10 people and no more than 32 people. Divide participants into subgroups of 5-8 people. The goal is to have at least two subgroups, but no more than four.

Materials: Flip chart with markers

Background: Stories and narratives have been proven as a powerful method to organize information and deal with complexity. Major corporations, such as 3M and Royal Dutch/Shell use storytelling and scenarios techniques to analyze their changing environment, envision the future, and develop strategic and business plans.

Traditional techniques for understanding trends, such as forced ranking and cross-impact analysis grids, are valuable tools. However, by themselves, they are not sufficient to capture the full richness and implications of the future. Storytelling has a number of advantages:

- It is an intuitively comfortable approach for most people and, therefore, the easiest and most productive way to begin analyzing the trends.

- It presents findings in a real-world context rather than an artificial or purely theoretical one.

- They are memorable, making it easier for board and staff to remember the essential points.

- They engage the board and staff by capturing their imagination and creating a sense of excitement about the future.

- They capture the four key elements necessary for understanding the trends by defining: relationships, sequence of events, cause and effect, and priority among items.

Advance Reading Assignment: Have participants review trend information relevant to their association. This information may come from scanning activities their association already has conducted.

Instructions

30-40 mins. • Give participants the opportunity to review and discuss their reactions to the issues covered in *Exploring the Future* by asking them to consider the three questions below. Discuss each question separately, and capture their responses on a flip chart:

• What is missing in the document? From your vantage point, are there issues or changes that weren't covered?

• What are the biggest "a-has!" or insights you gained about the future? Are there "a-has!" or insights you've gleaned from other sources? Name where (books, articles, Web sites) or who (in or out of the nonprofit community).

• Is there anything in the document that made you say, "No way! I don't believe that will happen in the next two to five years"?

30 mins. • Break into small groups of 5-8 people.

• Ask each group to create two lists.

• Small groups:

• Divide a flip chart sheet into two columns: Mark the left-hand column *Different in the World* and the right-hand column *Different for the Association*.

• Take 20 minutes to think about the trends and the discussion that just occurred. Consider:

– What will be different in the next 3-5 years?

– What will be different in the world in terms of social, demographic, economic, technological, or political trends?

– What will be different for our association?

• Record the group's observations in the appropriate columns in the flip chart.

TIP: *Remind participants to work quickly and intuitively. They should concentrate on naming the issues. They do not have to explain or defend their choices.*

- In the next 10 minutes, each small group should review the results and pick the top three issues. Mark the top three issues with an asterisk.

30-40 mins. • Participants remain in their small groups to create a "mini-story" about the future.

- Distribute "Storytelling" instructions handout.

- Small groups:

  - Create a headline that describes the future. The mini-story will flow from there.

  - Look at the issues chosen as the most critical.

  - Find ways these trends are interrelated (*i.e.*, the story must demonstrate the relationship among the three trends).

  - Reflect on the unique aspects of the association as revealed by the five association characteristics.

  - Ensure the story takes place at least two years from now but no more than five years from today.

  - Paint a scenario that is significantly different than today (*i.e.*, it is surprising, unexpected, unanticipated).

  - Make sure the story is plausible; it is based on facts and results from changes we know are occurring. While it may be surprising, the story is not meant as fiction or fantasy.

- Each small group tells its story to the entire group. The story should take 1 minute to tell.

60+ mins. • The entire group reconvenes.

- Each small group is allocated 2 minutes to name its top three issues and tell its mini-story (including the headline). All groups must report out before any discussion is allowed.

- After all the small groups have told their stories, the entire panel engages in a free-flowing discussion of what they have learned. Here are some sample questions to guide the large-group discussion:

  - What do we agree on? What common themes or insights emerged in each of the mini-stories?

- Where do we diverge? What different themes or ideas emerged in one story but not the others? Why did those divergent themes emerge? What assumptions led the subgroups to interpret the future differently?

- What's missing? Stepping back and looking at all the stories, is there something missing that needs to be included or considered? What is it?

- What mega-opportunities for the association do the participants see in their mini-stories?

- What threats or issues of concern for the association do the participants see in their mini-stories?

- Which trends warrant further investigation or monitoring?

Exercise 4
Asking Questions About the Future

Because the future is uncertain, it is more important to ask the "right" questions than to strive for ever-changing "right" answers. This exercise will help you develop a frame of reference that will enable you to ask more probing questions about your association's future.

Part I. Imagine you are a time traveler. You are going back five years into the past to visit with the board and staff of your association. You will be helping them prepare for their future (which is your today!).

Also imagine that, as a time traveler, you are bound to obey the "Time Travelers' Directive." This directive prohibits you from revealing what their future may hold. You are not allowed to speak about any future facts or events. However, you are allowed to assist your board and staff by helping them figure out the right questions to ask about their future.

Imagine you are back at your association five years ago. Think about what the world was like then. What was happening in your organization? Among your members? What events occurring five years ago might have given you cues about today, if you had carefully considered them?

What questions *could* you have asked back then, but didn't?

Example: We see many corporations going through major changes, such as downsizing, training for new skills, and adopting new technologies. How might these changes affect what our members expect from us?

Part II. Now, let's travel back to the present. Guess what? A time traveler from five years in the future has come to visit your association! What clues and cues might he provide?

What questions might he use to lead your board and staff into the future?

Example: What demands will be placed on our association as more and more Gen X-ers enter into our profession or trade?

What might be the impact on our membership services capabilities? Our communications structure? Our governance process?

Part III. Look at the list of questions from Part II:

- What are the common elements in the questions listed?

  - Based on these questions, what are two or three future forces or trends you believe to be "critical uncertainties" because:

    – They will have a major impact on your association's future; and

    – It is too soon to know how the future will unfold in response to them.

- What additional questions about the future come to mind when you look at the list?

- Are there any other cues or clues your association is missing?

Exercise 4A

The Time Travelers Exercise
Learning How To Ask Questions About the Future

Objective: To develop participants' ability to ask more probing questions about the association's future. This is a fun exercise to help participants change their frame of reference.

Time: 65-85 minutes

Format: Small groups of 4-8 each

Materials: Flip chart, markers, masking tape, and handouts of these instructions and "Asking Questions About the Future"

Instructions

5 mins.
- Review the objective for the exercise with the group.
- Form small groups of 4-8.
- Small groups select a recorder and a reporter.
- Distribute copies of these instructions and "Asking Questions About the Future."

10-15 mins.
- Tell participants to read the introduction and Part I of the worksheet on "Asking Questions About the Future."
- Review the following instruction for the *first* small group discussion and report-backs.
- Small groups make a list of at least *five* questions about your association's future you could have asked five years ago—knowing what you know today.

10-15 mins.
- Ask the reporter from each group one of their questions.
- Record the question on the flip chart.
- Repeat this sequence until all the questions are recorded:
  - Noting questions developed by more than one group.
  - Beginning with a different small group each round.

10-15 mins. • Tell participants to read Part II of the worksheet on "Asking Questions About the Future."

• Review the following instruction for the *second* round of small group discussions and report-backs.

• Ask participants if they have any questions about what to do.

• Small groups make a list of at least *five* questions that can be used to lead your board and staff into the future.

10-15 mins. • Ask the reporter from each group one of their questions.

• Record the question on the flip chart.

• Repeat this sequence until all the questions are recorded:

  • Noting questions developed by more than one group.

  • Beginning with a different small group each round.

20 mins. • Post the compiled list of questions about your association's future for clear viewing.

• Discuss the topics under Part III in "Asking Questions About the Future."

• Record participants' ideas on the flip chart.

Exercise 5
Four Jobs of the Future

Look around organizations today and really ask what needs to be done to build and sustain an enterprise capable of innovation, adaptation, daring and speed? What is needed to truly build an enterprise where people are treated as the strategic assets that almost all organizations claim they are? Contributing writer Richard Wilkinson, whose most recent career had him the director of Human Resources for a medium-size enterprise, dreamed up four jobs needed in the future and described their key characteristics.

NOTES:

[1] Dick Davis in Joel Barker's video *The Business of Paradigms* (1990)

[2] Jeffrey Pfeffer, *The Human Equation*, Boston: Harvard University Press (1998)

[3] Lester Thurow, Dean, MIT's Sloan School of Management, in keynote address to AMA Human Resources Management conference, Boston (1993)

[4] William Bridges, *Managing Transitions*, Reading, MA: Addison-Wesley (1991)

ABOUT RICHARD WILKINSON

Over 25 years experience in human resources management, consulting, leadership and teaching. HR director for the City of Redmond, Washington, 1985 to 2000. Instructor in Human Resources Management at the University of Washington. Life-certified as a Senior Professional in Human Resources (SPHR). Richard can be reached at: rcwseattle@home.com

NOTE: This article first appeared on www.futurist.com

Four Jobs of the Future

	Collaborative Futurist	Chief People Strategist	Learning Evangelist	Transition Champion
Clarion Call	"No corporation today gets hit by the future between the eyes; they get it in the temple."[1]	"People are the strategy."[2]	"If natural resources can be bought, capital can be borrowed, and technology can be copied, what are you left with as the only source of long run strategic competitive advantage? The skills of your work force. There is nothing else…nothing at all."[3]	"It isn't the changes that do you in, it's the transitions."[4]
Heart of the Job	Identifies emerging trends and explores implications with teams as integral part of strategic planning process. Builds scenarios to facilitate understanding.	Champions, nurtures, and facilitates implementation of high performance people strategies in collaboration with organization's leaders.	Installs multifaceted learning practices throughout organization consistent with its strategic priorities.	Works with teams at all levels in guiding them through emotional and technical adaptations associated with desirable or necessary changes.
Focus	System-wide	Executive leadership	Teams; Individual performance	Teams; Individual performance
Deliverables	Briefings Scenarios Plans Monitoring processes Progress Reports	Learning events Policies Implementation plans & timelines Feedback Loops	Learning practices Management Indoctrination Learning "Triggers"	Transition education Transition Strategies Monitoring processes Meeting facilitation Individual coaching
Metrics	Plan attainment Plan refinements Trend credibility	Organization performance Adoption patterns Feedback from field	Implementation of new practices Innovation rate Organization performance	Teams helped Length of time to fully implement change Feedback from Field
Metaphor	Wizard	Visionary	Teacher	Healer
Must Read	*Futurist* Magazine	*The Human Equation*	*The Fifth Discipline*	*Managing Transitions*

Appendix H

ASAE Foundation Futures Scan
Community of Practice Guest Experts
(in order of participation)

Christopher Dede, Ed.D.

Co-Director, Technology in Education Program, Harvard University

I think the key to understanding mediated communication is that it complements face-to-face interaction rather than substituting for it. This is typical of the whole history of media (e.g., writing did not displace speech). Possibilities for face-to-face interactions among members of professional associations are scant in comparison to their professional lives; for associations to look for powerful ways to supplement direct human contact makes sense.

For more about Christopher Dede, see
http://hugse7.harvard.edu/gsedata/resource_pkg.profile?rowid_in=0000123C.000A.0060.

For links to Dede's papers see
http://www.virtual.gmu.edu/SS_research/cdpapers/index.htm.

Douglass Carmichael, Ph.D.

Co-Owner, bigmindmedia.com; Founder, Critical Humanities Institute; Pioneer, On-line Communities

My feeling is that between business and the market, and government, which is fading in its importance, the individual is left rather isolated and associations might be one of the most important ways to find our way towards new kinds of governance. Only associations, which can speak for the collective needs of a large membership, when those needs are not exactly aligned with the market, can probably make a difference in modifying raw market trends. Both for the good of the member businesses, and for the citizens, and for society, this might be an important emerging role.

For more about Douglass Carmichael, see
http://www.tmn.com/~doug/.

Ernest Sternberg, Ph.D.

Associate Professor of Planning, School of Architecture and Planning, State University of New York at Buffalo; Author, *The Economy of Icons*

Already, I sense the beginnings of a new movement, more profound even than the environmental movement: a movement for the preservation and adaptive reuse of direct human experience. It is here that "associations" have their particular task. If they live up to the promise in their name, they will be agents that help us re-associate. Where we live in electronically charged alienation, perhaps they will find ways to help us find, meet, challenge, and learn from each other, in each others' presence, again.

For more about Ernest Sternberg, see
http://info.greenwood.com/books/0275966/0275966410.html.

James Dator, Ph.D.

Head, Alternative Futures Graduate Option, University of Hawaii's Department of Political Science; Director, Hawaii Research Center for Future Studies

In my consulting, I always ask an organization to spend some time contemplating their past—understanding it, respecting it, and asking themselves, seriously, whether there is any reason (other than their own job!) why the organization should continue or not. That question cannot really be answered, however, until you have thought about what lies ahead. There may be renewed reason for organizations to live in the future not readily apparent in the present. Or there may be good reasons to let the organization die.

For more about James Dator, see
http://www.soc.hawaii.edu/future/.

Ken Dychtwald, Ph.D.

President and CEO, Age Wave, LLC; Author, *Age Wave, Bodymind,* and *Age Power: How the 21st Century Will be Ruled by the New Old*

I completely agree that in a longer life, we will need to repeatedly be retrained and in all likelihood, re-inspired in our work-lives. Learning institutions and employers will need to do an even better job of this than they're doing at present. Yes, this might cause associations to change in many ways, but perhaps this change would be for the better as it would institutionalize the continual rekindling of corporate and individual fires so necessary in our modern world.

For more about Ken Dychtwald, see
http://www.agewave.com/agewave/dychtwald.html.

William Strauss

Co-Founder, Capitol Steps; Co-author, *Generations, The Fourth Turning, Millennials Rising: The Next Great Generation*

The tendency of Millennials to "associate" does not at all mean that existing associations have an easy path ahead. Many of the new Millennial associational genres involve new technologies, new interests, new causes, new corners of the culture. Older people (especially those still pursuing grand causes) may be frustrated with how these kids pay scant attention to those old causes and instead cut through to something new. Goodbye, Kiwanis. Hello, Buddy Lists. The smart association will be one that finds a way to tap into the distinctly "modern," 21st-Century aspect of this new generational mindset. You may need to step aside a little, and let them organize a few things their own way.

For more about William Strauss, see
http://www.millenialsrising.com.

Jonathan Peck

Vice-President, Institute for Alternative Futures; Vice-President, Alternative Futures Associates

DO NOT WAIT FOR THE FUTURE. CREATE IT! The opportunity for associations is here and now. The Silent and Boomer generations are not monolithic, and they offer sets of needs and potentials that association leaders can work with even while preparing for the demands and talents of Gen X and Millennials. If I were an association exec looking at my budget, I'd want to assure myself that I was spending at least a small proportion on developing young leaders.

For more about Jonathan Peck, see
http://www.altfutures.com.

Jennifer Jarratt

Senior Vice-President, Coates & Jarratt, Inc.; Co-Author, *The Future at Work, Future Work*, and *Managing Your Future as an Association*

A lifelong connection to an association will mean integrating work and non-work in new ways that are different from traditional volunteerism and office-holding which often come towards the end of a work career. If we know we will have many more years to play with and we don't have to do all of our work time at once, then we are more likely to take breaks in the middle and do something that furthers our profession, our interests, or our concerns. We might need associations to help us make our time out be a bridge between one kind of work and another, or to be a significant life activity that we can pursue with different intensity and hours at different times in our lives. We may see many more associations developing to meet our non-professional needs and interests.

For more about Jennifer Jarratt, see
http://www.coatesandjarratt.com/.

Paul Ray, Ph.D.

Executive Vice-President, American LIVES, Inc.; Co-Author, *The Cultural Creatives: How 50 Million People are Changing the World*

Sherry Ruth Anderson, Ph.D.

Former Head of Psychological Research, Clarke Institute of Psychiatry; Co-Author, *The Cultural Creatives: How 50 Million People Are Changing the World*

It is very likely that many associations who are associated with good causes will be seeing the Cultural Creatives (CCs), because they are much more likely to be volunteers and contributors than the rest of the population. Cultural Creatives got to be that way because they identify with many of the altruistic causes of the last 40 years, right up to the WTO demonstrations in Seattle: civil rights, peace, women's, jobs and social justice, environment, ecology, alternative health care, organic food, personal and spiritual growth, global issues, etc. They are less likely to be interested in culturally conservative associations, or those associations whose primary concerns are making money. CCs will favor associations that state and try to live up to idealistic purposes

For more about Paul Ray and Sherry Ruth Anderson, see
http://www.culturalcreatives.org.

Allen Hammond, Ph.D.

Senior Scientist and Director of Strategic Analysis, World Resources Institute; Author, *Which World? Global Destinies, Regional Choices*

But I do think that many organizations can come together to form a local-global structure. Some other people call this a network organization. By whatever name, its a realization that to deal with global issues, we need to work with others who have their own special local knowledge and create something that is larger than the sum of the parts. Not that its easy—Global Forest Watch has some 90 different organizations as participating members, and we're only in 6 countries so far. It would be interesting to imagine a similar link-up among national associations around the world on important issues, whether free trade or fair labor practices.

For more about Allen Hammond, see
http://www.wri.org.

Michael Shuman

Former Co-Director, the Institute for Policy Studies; Author, *Going Local: Creating Self-Reliant Communities in a Global Age, Towards a Global Village*

If I were the head of a national foundation, I would finance projects that demonstrated and spread state-of-the-art studies, policies, and technologies promoting local self-reliance. If I were the head of a professional association or industry group, I would try to help my constituents expand their market share locally. I'd try to figure out if there were particular obstacles to my constituents competing effectively in their own backyard (such as the absence of health insurance for small businesses) and seek to mobilize appropriate-scale remedies (like pool insurance purchasing). If I were the head of an advocacy organization, I'd fight for: an elimination of all kinds of federal subsidies, tax programs, and other benefits that support non-local businesses; the wholesale devolution of power, responsibility, and money to the local level; the reconfiguring of our constitution to revive the Tenth Amendment.

For more about Michael Shuman, see
http://www.tni.org/fellows/shuman.htm.

Sohail Inayatullah, Ph.D.

Political Scientist and Professor of Futures Studies, IMC; Visiting Professor, Queensland University of Technology

Anticipatory action learning means creating new ideas and actions based on conversations with others, that is, making changes based not on expert ideas but on issues that employees or other groups you are working with raise. It is a constant back and forth cycle where ideas are refined through discussion. However, anticipatory action learning is also focused on asking questions about the future—the entire range of preferred, probable, possible as well as the layers of the future. The point for associations would be to be explicit on your image of the future.

For more about Sohail Inayatullah, see
http://www.google.com/search?q=sohail+inayatullah.

Walter Truett Anderson, Ph.D.

Vice President, Meridian International Institute; Associate Editor and Columnist, Pacific News Service; Author, *Reality Isn't What It Used to Be* and *The Future of the Self*

The world is made up of a lot of systems—economic, political, cultural, biological. No living system is entirely closed—it has to have some inputs and outputs with its environment—but in the past some systems, such as remote tribal societies, local economies, and ecosystems were much more closed than they are now. What's happening now, with the increase in mobility of people and symbols, is that all kinds of systems are changing their boundaries and/or establishing new connections with other systems.

For more about Walter Truett Anderson, see
http://www.google.com/search?q=walter+truett+anderson&hl=en&lr=&safe=off.

Scott Beaty
Team Leader, Group Leadership and Performance, Royal Dutch/Shell

I don't think the aspiration (of associations) ought to be to create a learning organization; the aspiration ought to be to create the organization of the future that honors the values of its members.

If I was a national association I would want to be learning about two things real quick…how is my association going to be affected by globalization? And how could my association develop and leverage our diverse capabilities to the advantages of our members.

Judy Smith, Ph.D.
Web Diva, sitetrainer.com; Chair, Online MIS Program, University of Phoenix; Vice President of Instructional Development, CertiLearn, Inc.

The biggest challenge in becoming a true learning organization is that we live in an age of instant gratification. To fundamentally reorient ourselves as individuals and organizations, especially when it comes to distance learning, is not a task that will be done overnight. It will take years.

For more about Judy Smith, see
http://www.sitetrainer.com.

Appendix I

Additional Acknowledgements

The ASAE Foundation appreciates the contribution of the thought leaders who participated in the futures scan online community of practice, focus groups, surveys, chapter reviews, and telephone interviews.

Futures Scan Community of Practice

Mark Anderson, CAE, Executive Director, American Society for Surgery of the Hand, Rosemont, Ill.

Michael Anderson, CAE, President/CEO, Canadian Society of Association Executives, Toronto, Ontario, Canada

Adrienne Ash, Assistant Staff Vice President, National Association of Home Builders, Washington, D.C.

Janet Bray, CAE, Executive Director, National Association of Enrolled Agents, Gaithersburg, Md.

Joan Campbell, Executive Vice President, Home Sewing Association, New York, N.Y.

Virgil Carter, Executive Director, Project Management Institute, Newton Square, Penn.

Linda Christopher, CAE, President/CEO, The Christopher Group, Santa Rosa, Calif.

Joanne Cole, CMP, CAE, Managing Member, Professional Management Association, LLC, Hillsborough, N.J.

Tom Conger, President, Social Technologies, Inc., Alexandria, Va.

Jeffrey Cufaude, Principal and Partner, like minded people, Indianapolis, Ind.

Susan Darrow, Consulting Partner, Information Systems Consulting Group, Inc., La Grange, Ill.

Patricia Digh, President, RealWork, Washington, D.C.

Jeff De Cagna, Managing Director, Strategic Learning and Development, Special Libraries Association, Washington, D.C.

Charles Deale, CAE, VP Member/Candidate Services, Association for Investment Management and Research, Charlottesville, Va.

Atul Dighe, Senior Futurist, Institute for Alternative Futures, Alexandria, Va.

Henry Ernstthal, JD, CAE, President, Ernstthal & Associates, Washington, D.C.

Lola Fehr, RN, MS, CAE, Executive Director, American Society of Bariatric Physicians, Englewood, Colo.

Mark J. Golden, CAE, Executive Director, National Court Reporters Association, Vienna, Va.

Debbera Hayward, Senior Director Corporate Diversity, American Red Cross, Falls Church, Va.

Jery Huntley, Executive Director, Vinyl Siding Institute, Washington, D.C.

Mark Justman, Futurist, Institute of Alternative Futures, Alexandria, Va.

Sherry Keramidas, Ph.D., CAE, Executive Director, Regulatory Affairs Professional Society, Rockville, Md.

Robin Kriegel, CAE, CEO/Executive Director, American Society for Parenteral & Enteral Nutrition, Silver Spring, Md.

Mary Krukoff, CAE, Director of Education, National Automatic Merchandising Association, Chicago, Ill.

Vinay Kumar, Owner, Franklins Printing & Mailing, Warrenton, Va.

Joan Carolyn Kuyper, CAE, Deputy Director, Society of Women Engineers, New York, N.Y.

James F. Linn, Jr., Director, American Gas Association, Washington, D.C.

Norm Linsky, Director of Marketing Research/Business Development, American College of Cardiology—National Headquarters, Bethesda, Md.

Erik Lofgren, Director Member Services, Regulatory Affairs Professional Society, Rockville, Md.

Michelle Mason, Vice President, Research Programs, American Society of Association Executives, Washington, D.C.

Janet McCallen, CAE, Executive Director, Financial Planning Association, Atlanta, Ga.

Jeffrey Morgan, CAE, Chief Operating Officer, Futures Industry Association, Washington, D.C.

D. Brent Mulgrew, Executive Director, Ohio State Medical Association, Hilliard, Ohio

Peter O'Neil, CAE, Group Leader Member Services, American Industrial Hygiene Association, Fairfax, Va.

Robert Olson, Research Director, Institute for Alternative Futures, Alexandria, Va.

Annette Petrick, CAE, President, Petrick Outsourcing Unlimited, Inc., Woodstock, Va.

Edward Potter, CAE, Director, Global Resource Center, American Society of Association Executives, Washington, D.C.

Marsha Rhea, CAE, Senior Associate, Institute for Alternative Futures, Alexandria, Va.

Mary Riemersma, CAE, Executive Director, California Association of Marriage and Family Therapists, San Diego, Calif.

Janice Rossi, Executive Director, North Carolina Association of Rehabilitation Facilities, Inc., Raleigh, N.C.

Nancy D. Safer, Ph.D., Executive Director, Council for Exceptional Children, Arlington, Va.

Frances Shuping, CAE, Vice President, Technology and Communications, Air Conditioning Contractors of America, Washington, D.C.

Barbara Sido, CAE, Managing Director, Professional Practice, American Institute of Architects, Washington, D.C.

Kimberly Svevo, CAE, Executive Director, International Society for the Prevention of Child Abuse & Neglect, Chicago, Ill.

Robert Teplansky, Principal, New Community Association, Northborough, Mass.

Sarah C. Varner, Executive Vice President/COO, American Society of Association Executives Foundation, Washington, D.C.

Association Executives Futures Scan Focus Group Participants

Janet Bray, CAE, Executive Vice President, National Association of Enrolled Agents, Gaithersburg, Md.

Myron Clack, CAE, President, Innovative Concepts, Richmond, Va.

John Cox, CAE, Executive Director, American Association of Pharmaceutical Scientists, Arlington, Va.

Thomas Dolan, Ph.D, FACHE, CAE, President/CEO, American College of Healthcare Executives, Chicago, Ill.

Mark Engle, CAE, Principal, Association Management Center, Glenview, Ill.

Michael Fleming, CAE, President, Equipment Leasing Association, Arlington, Va.

Mark J. Golden, CAE, Executive Director, National Court Reporters Association, Vienna, Va.

John Grau, CEO, National Electrical Contractors Association, Bethesda, Md.

J. Stephen Larkin, President, The Aluminum Association, Washington, D.C.

Neil Offen, CAE, President, Direct Selling Association, Washington, D.C.

Sarah Sanford, CAE, Executive Director, Society of Actuaries, Schaumburg, Ill.

Peg Scherbarth, Vice President Sales and Marketing, Interliant Association Solutions, Inc., Chantilly, Va.

Fredrick Spahr, CAE, Executive Director, American Speech, Language, Hearing Association, Rockville, Md.

Kendall Starkweather, Ph.D., Executive Director, International Technology Education Association, Reston, Va.

Lee VanBremen Ph.D, CAE, Executive Vice President, College of American Pathologists, Northfield, Ill.

Barbara Belmont, CAE, Executive Director, American School Food Service Association, Alexandria, Va.

Raymond Crabbs, Senior Vice President/COO, Points of Light Foundation, Washington, D.C.

Michael Davis, Executive Vice President, American Alliance for Health, Physical Education, Recreation & Dance, Reston, Va.

Diana Ewert, MPA, CAE, Managing Director, Member/Customer Operations, The Urban Land Institute, Washington, D.C.

David Gamse, Executive Director, Jewish Council for the Aging, Rockville, Md.

Anetha Grant, Vice President, Convention Sales/Marketing, Nashville Convention and Visitors Bureau, Nashville, Tenn.

Wayne Gross, CMP, CAE, Executive Director, Technical Association of Pulp & Paper Industry, Atlanta, Ga.

Barbara Byrd Keenan, CAE, President, Community Associations Institute, Alexandria, Va.

Linda Kloss, MA, RHIA, Executive Vice President and CEO, American Health Information Management Association, Chicago, Ill.

Robin Kriegel, CAE, CEO/Executive Director, American Society for Parenteral and Enteral Nutrition, Silver Spring, Md.

Cynthia Lund, Vice President State Society Affairs/Strategic Planning, American Institute of Certified Public Accountants, Washington, D.C.

Ronald Moen, Executive Director, American Association of Orthodontists, St. Louis, Mo.

Tonya Muse, Executive Director, Envelope Manufacturers Association Foundation, Alexandria, Va.

Ann Western, CPA, CFP, CAE, Vice President Finance/Administration and CFO, American Forest & Paper Association, Washington, D.C.

Consultants Futures Scan Focus Group Participants

Rhea Blanken, President, Results Technology, Inc., Bethesda, Md.

Catherine Bower, CAE, President, Cate Bower Communications, West River, Md.

Bruce Butterfield, CAE, President/CEO, The Forbes Group, Fairfax, Va.

Stephen Carey, Ph.D., CAE, President, Association Marketing and Management Resources, Bethesda, Md.

Jill Cornish, President/Publisher, Association Trends, Bethesda, Md.

Cynthia D'Amour, President, People Power Unlimited, Ann Arbor, Mich.

James Dalton, CAE, President, Strategic Counsel, Derwood, Md.

Richard Dorman, CAE, President/CEO, The Catalyst Group, Alexandria, Va.

Douglas Eadie, President, Doug Eadie Presents!, Frisco, Texas

Henry Ernstthal, JD, CAE, President, Ernstthal & Associates, Washington, D.C.

Andrew Lang, CPA, President/CEO, Lang Group Chartered, Bethesda, Md.

Donald R. (Chip) Levy, Principal, The Rochelle Organization, Inc., Washington, D.C.

Ginger Nichols, CAE, President, GinCommGroup, San Francisco, Calif.

J. P. O'Connor, Principal, O'Connor Management Consulting and Training, Burbank, Calif.

Steven Worth, Senior Partner, Plexus Consulting Group, Washington, D.C.

A special acknowledgement to the focus group participants at the ASAE Management and Technology Conference in Indianapolis (1999), ASAE Orlando 2000, ASAE Management and Technology Conference in Washington, D.C. (2000).

A special thank you to the following reviewers:

Mark Levin, CSP, CAE, President, BAI, Inc., Columbia, Md., Author, *Millennium Membership* (ASAE 1999)

Bruce Tulgan, President, Rainmaker Thinking, Inc., New Haven, Conn.

Ann Mahoney, CAE, Vice President, Electronic Communication and Technology, American Society of Association Executives, Washington, D.C.

Paul Pomerantz, CAE, Executive Director, Society of Cardiovascular & Interventional Radiology, Fairfax, Va.

Marcie Granahan, CAE, Vice President, Member Services, American Society of Association Executives, Washington, D.C.

Edward Potter, CAE, Director, Global Resource Center, American Society of Association Executives, Washington, D.C.

John Donaldson, International Section Manager, American Society of Association Executives, Washington, D.C.

Special thank you to Donald R. "Chip" Levy, principal of The Rochelle Organization, Inc., for his insight and guidance during the development of this publication. The Rochelle Organization is a consulting practice based in Washington, D.C., specializing in education and knowledge development and providing strategic program and product planning consulting services to the nonprofit community. For more information, e-mail troinc@aol.com.

The ASAE Foundation staff liaison was Michelle Mason, vice president, Foundation Research Programs.

Thank you to our donors

The futures scan and other research related projects are supported by two capital campaigns, which have raised over $10 million. The ASAE Foundation wishes to acknowledge the donors to the most recent campaign, Partners for the Future:

CORPORATE DONORS

Diamond Founding Partners

Marriott Hotels Resorts & Suites

Starwood Hotels & Resorts Worldwide

Platinum Partners

Hilton Hotels Corporation

Hyatt Hotels Corporation

MBNA America

Opryland Hospitality Group

Gold Partners

American Airlines

Delta Air Lines

Fairmont Hotels & Resorts

First Union National Bank

Loews Hotels/CNA Insurance

Mohegan Sun

SunTrust Bank

United Airlines

Wyndham Hotels & Resorts

Silver Partners

AON

The Broadmoor

Colonial Williamsburg Hotel & Resort

Component Graphics Inc.

Galaxy Information Services, LLC

GES Expo Services

Hershey Resorts

Jenner & Block

Langan Associates, PC

Outrigger Hotels & Resorts

The Peabody Orlando

Ritz-Carlton Hotel Company LLC

Tate & Tryon, CPAs & Consultants

Walt Disneyworld Resort and Disneyland Resort

Bronze Partners

Associated Luxury Hotels

Avis Rent a Car Systems, Inc.

Bank of America

Boca Raton Resort and Club

CTE Associates

The Cloisters Hotel

ConferenceDirect

Legg Mason

Peabody Memphis

PGA National Resort and Spa

Precision Meetings & Events

ASSOCIATION & INDIVIDUAL DONORS

Diamond Founding Partners

APICS The Educational Society for Resource Management

American Society of Association Executives

Founding Partners

American Medical Association

Million Dollar Round Table

Platinum Partners

American Association of Orthodontists

American College of Healthcare Executives

American Diabetes Association

American Heart Association

Arthritis Foundation

Bostrom Corporation

Credit Union Execs Society

Golf Course Superintendents Association

Marilynn & Michael S. Olson, CAE

Points of Light Foundation

Produce Marketing Association

Texas Hospital Association

Gold Partners

American Academy of Ophthalmology

American Academy of Orthopaedic Surgeons

American College of Cardiology

American College of Emergency Physicians

American Forest & Paper Association

American Gas Association

American Petroleum Institute

American School Food Service Association

American Society of Civil Engineers

American Society of Mechanical Engineers

American Urological Association

ASAE Staff

Association Management Group, Inc.

Association Management Services

College of American Pathologists

Door & Hardware Institute

Fernley & Fernley

Jerald A. Jacobs, Esq.

Barbara Byrd Keenan, CAE & Terrence Keenan

National Association of College Stores

National Electrical Contractors Association

National Paint & Coatings Association

National Roofing Contractors Association

National Speakers Association

Ginger Nichols, CAE—GinCommGroup

Semiconductor Equipment & Materials Intl

TAPPI—The Technical Association of the Pulp & Paper Industry

Texas Restaurant Association

Silver Partners

American Academy of Family Physicians

American Academy of Physical Medicine & Rehabilitation

American Association of Medical Society Executives

American College of Chest Physicians

American College of Rheumatology

Association Management Center

Linda Chandler, CAE

College of American Pathologists

John B. Cox, CAE

Joan Cutlip-Spivey

Dairy Council of Wisconsin Inc

Curtis C. Deane, CFRE, CAE

Anne DeCicco, CAE

Patricia Digh

Susan and Robert J. Dolibois, CAE

Drohan Management Group

Ernst & Young Association Management

Edison Electric Institute

Family Motor Coach Association

Richard B. Green

Wayne Gross, CAE

Gay Holden

Iowa Society of Association Executives

Gary LaBranche, CAE

Luggage & Leather Goods Manufacturers

Ronald S. Moen

Kenneth E. Monroe

National Association of Enrolled Agents

National Society of Fund Raising Executives

Printing Industries of America

Professional Liability Underwriting Society

Marsha Rhea, CAE

Judy & Colin Rorrie Jr., Ph.D., CAE

Sarah Sanford, CAE

Texas Society of Association Execs

Todd Wurschmidt, Ph.D., CAE

Sarah C. Varner

CONVENTION & VISITORS BUREAUS

Diamond Partners

Las Vegas CVA

Chicago CTB/Metropolitan Pier & Expo Authority

Founding Partners

Anaheim/Orange County VCB

Greater Miami CVB

Hawaii CVB

Los Angeles CVB

NYC & Company CVB

San Diego CVB

Platinum Partners

Atlanta CVB

CVB of Greater Cleveland

CVB of Greater Kansas City

Dallas CVB

Denver CVB

Greater Boston CVB

Greater Phoenix CVB

Indianapolis CVA

Long Beach Area CVB

Louisville & Jefferson County CVB

Milwaukee CVB

Minneapolis CVB

Nashville CVB

Orlando/Orange County CVB

Puerto Rico Visitors Bureau

San Jose CVB

Seattle King County CVB

St. Louis CVC

Washington, D.C., CVA

Gold Partners

Bloomington CVB

Charlotte CVB

Greater Columbus CVB

Greater Pittsburgh CVB

Greater Metropolitan Detroit CVB

And nearly 100 other individuals and organizations.

Appendix J

About the Institute for Alternative Futures

The Institute for Alternative Futures (IAF) guides associations, corporations, and governments to take steps today to align their future with their highest aspirations. As a futurist think tank, IAF monitors demographic and economic trends, value and attitude shifts, and emerging technologies across a diverse client base. As consulting futurists, IAF uses a range of techniques to help organizations think effectively about the future they prefer to create. Established in 1977, today IAF is a recognized and respected consulting futurist firm for organizations as diverse as:

- **Associations**—American Society of Association Executives Foundation, Electrical Contracting Foundation, American Institute of Architects, American Cancer Society, Pharmaceutical Research and Manufacturers of America, Regulatory Affairs Professional Society, American Society for Quality, American Public Transportation Association, and Planned Parenthood Federation of America.

- **Government**—U.S. Department of Defense, U.S. Department of Health and Human Services Health Resources and Services Agency (HRSA), U.S. Environmental Protection Agency, World Health Organization, more than 30 states and many cities, including St. Louis, Mo. and Peoria, Ill.

- **Corporations**—Johnson and Johnson, Mead Corp., Monsanto, AT&T, British Telecom, Vivendi, Bayer, Pfizer, GlaxoWellcome, and SmithKline Beecham. (Through IAF's for-profit subsidiary, Alternative Futures Associates.)

The ASAE Foundation commissioned IAF to conduct its 2000–2001 environmental scan to explore emerging issues for associations. IAF worked with hundreds of association executives in face-to-face and online forums to identify the seven ideas featured in this report. IAF also drew on its own team of futurists on its network of provocative thinkers to resource this scan. The ASAE Futures Scan Team of IAF researchers and writers includes the following individuals:

Robert Olson, IAF research director and project director for the ASAE Foundation Futures Scan. Before joining IAF, Olson was a project director and consultant to the director at the Office of Technology Assessment of the U.S. Congress. His areas of expertise include technology, environment, health, transportation, and urban design. He is helping create a network of futurists working throughout the federal government. He is the editor of *Mending the Earth: A World for Our Grandchildren* and co-author of the textbook *Time's Harvest: Exploring the Future.* He has a masters and Ph.D. from the University of Michigan.

Atul Dighe, senior futurist. Before joining IAF, Dighe worked for the futures research firm of Coates & Jarratt. He is skilled in developing futures programs and workshops for diverse clients. He has extensive experience in strategic planning, organizational development, and facilitation. He graduated from the University of Houston-Clear Lake with a masters of science in studies of the future.

Mark Justman, futurist. Justman came to IAF with a background in public policy and governance, having worked for three years as a researcher and policy analyst at the Hawaii State Legislature. He has analyzed and described trends for a variety of corporate, nonprofit, and public-sector organizations. He received his masters degree at the Futures Studies Program in the Political Science Department of the University of Hawaii.

Jennifer Kang, futurist. Before joining IAF, Kang was a program analyst at the Maternal and Child Health Bureau, a division of the Health Resources and Services Administration. She has managed projects for IAF, including several for health professionals and pharmaceutical organizations. She earned her masters in health sciences in health policy from Johns Hopkins University.

Tom Conger, futurist and founder, Social Technologies, LLC. Conger worked for the futurist firm Coates & Jarrett before joining IAF. He continues to be an IAF associate. He graduated from the University of Houston-Clear Lake with a masters of science in studies of the future.

VISION STATEMENT

The ASAE Foundation will be the global leader enabling associations, their executives, and their partners to prepare for the future.

MISSION STATEMENT

The ASAE Foundation, in partnership with ASAE, is dedicated to enhancing the association community's ability to anticipate and prepare for change through education and research, thereby maximizing the community's positive impact on society.